How To Do
English
and Verbal
Reasoning

CEM
(Durham University)

OXFORD

UNIVERSITY PRESS

Great Clarendon Street, Oxford, OX2 6DP, United Kingdom

Oxford University Press is a department of the University of Oxford.
It furthers the University's objective of excellence in research, scholarship,
and education by publishing worldwide. Oxford is a registered trade
mark of Oxford University Press in the UK and in certain other countries

British Library Cataloguing in Publication Data

Data available

978-0-1927-4288-9

10 9 8 7

Paper used in the production of this book is a natural, recyclable product
made from wood grown in sustainable forests. The manufacturing process
conforms to the environmental regulations of the country of origin.

Printed in China

Acknowledgements

Page make-up: Oxford Designers & Illustrators
Illustrations: Beehive Illustration
Cover illustrations: Lo Cole

Although we have made every effort to trace and contact all copyright holders
before publication this has not been possible in all cases. If notified, the
publisher will rectify any errors or omissions at the earliest opportunity.

Links to third party websites are provided by Oxford in good faith and for
information only. Oxford disclaims any responsibility for the materials
contained in any third party website referenced in this work.

Contents

Introduction   4-7

Parent tips and information   8–10

1 Comprehension   11–32

A Spotting
B Inference and deduction
C Vocabulary
D Text types
E Spelling rules
F Literary effects

2 Vocabulary   33–52

A Synonyms grid
B Antonyms grid
C Words most similar
D Words most opposite
E Words matching pairs of words
F Odd words out
G Logical reasoning

3 Cloze tests   53–74

A Find the three-letter word
B Find the three letters
C Complete a word
D Contextual words
E Selecting words in sentences
F Selecting words in paragraphs
G Vocabulary understanding
H Superfluous words

4 Mixed grammar   75–87

A Singular and plural
B Root words
C Word classes
D Tenses

How do you prepare for the exam?   88–91

Glossary   92–93

Answers   94–99

Resources   100

Standard 11⁺ English and Verbal Reasoning Test
(Central pull-out section)

Introduction

The CEM test is a different style to the GL Assessment tests that have been used in the 11[+] selective examinations. The test has been created to be 'tutor-proof' in order to create a fairer system for children sitting their entrance exams for many grammar and independent secondary schools. The English element of the exam will be recognisable from the curriculum that your child will have covered in school, but the verbal reasoning is not a curriculum subject.

What is the CEM Exam?

Since the late 1990s, the Centre for Evaluation and Monitoring, as part of Durham University, has become a leading provider of 11[+] assessment. It aims to provide fair assessments and accurate testing to identify those children who are more academically capable. They aim to provide an ever-changing exam format with timed sections covering a mixture of English, verbal reasoning, maths and non-verbal reasoning. In our experience we have found that there are two exams, which are sat on the same day and each last for 45 minutes with 15 minutes of preparation. Each test is divided into sections that are explained through an audio soundtrack. By creating changeable sections, unpredictable question types, intensity of speed and high vocabulary levels, CEM does provide an alternative to other 11[+] exams.

So is the CEM test 'tutor-proof'?

No book can tell you exactly what will be on the CEM examination paper so it is not possible for any book to teach your child how to jump through an exam hoop. With Bond, we don't believe in simply jumping through exam hoops, as we have spent over 50 years producing quality books and resources that teach children real skills and give them the knowledge and confidence to succeed in any exam. Bond welcomes the emphasis on holistic education and supporting school-based learning.

The skills and techniques needed for the CEM exam are the skills and techniques that underpin this range of books and papers. By following the books, test papers and this *How To Do* guide, your child will have a range of knowledge and techniques to help answer any English and verbal reasoning exam questions. Although there is no guarantee that these questions will come up on every paper, or indeed on any paper, what this book will provide is a solid foundation and a broad spectrum of techniques and knowledge. In summary, this book will provide a vital resource for all children preparing for the CEM 11[+] exam.

Is the CEM paper standard format or multiple-choice?

At the time of writing, it was not possible to confirm what format the CEM exams will take for any specific school, but from the experience of pupils who have already sat the paper, it would appear that there may be elements of both formats. It is usually easier for an exam board to offer multiple choice as papers can then be optically marked. Note though that a child who can do well in standard format tends to find the multiple-choice paper easier, whereas a child who has only covered a multiple-choice format will find the standard format significantly harder.

Bond prefers to use standard format books with a choice of standard and multiple-choice exam papers. This is to ensure that children have solid skills and techniques under their belt rather than an over-reliance on multiple-choice format skills. The CEM board are keen to stress their desire to mix the questions up and so the Bond CEM style books aim to encourage a child to think of how the same information could be presented in different ways. This is to encourage the logical skills required to deal with any question type that comes up on an exam paper.

What skills does this book cover?

This book will provide information, techniques, practice exercises and top tips in a wide range of key English and verbal reasoning areas as follows:

- **Comprehension skills**
  The most critical skills in comprehension, from spotting, inference and deduction to vocabulary building, spelling rules, text types and literary effects.

- **Vocabulary skills**
  The most critical skills in vocabulary building, from antonyms and synonyms to matching words, odd words out and logic questions.

- **Cloze test skills**
  The most critical skills in solving cloze tests, such as selecting words, superfluous words, completing words and placing words in context.

- **Mixed grammar skills**
  Underpinning skills that support all English and verbal reasoning questions, such as singular and plural words, root words, word classifications and tenses.

How can you use this book?

This book is designed for use by children and parents to help prepare for a CEM 11+ exam. It includes a range of top tips and suggestions. A wide range of question styles that may be found on the CEM test paper are presented with techniques and information to help answer the questions. This book provides a step-by-step tutorial that can be worked through from start to finish. It will become a reference tool to look up question types with which your child might struggle, with examples provided to explain how they are solved. The book covers a wide range of question types that can also complement other exams and will work in conjunction with the range of English and verbal reasoning CEM books and exam papers.

Why use this book?

How To Do CEM English and Verbal Reasoning is part of the long-established and well-known Bond series. The Bond range has been used for over 50 years and has been trusted by thousands of pupils, parents, teachers and tutors. This heritage provides confidence and a full range of supporting materials and resources.

A key strength with the Bond books is that all of the key skills build up gradually and are consolidated in each paper. Instead of learning one skill and then moving on to another, the Bond books have the same question types in each paper, which builds in consolidation. Instead of reaching the end of a book having forgotten the skills learnt, the Bond books keep each skill fresh. In order to learn each technique, this book gives an explanation and then several example questions. There is the opportunity for children to practise each technique, with regular recaps for children to consolidate each technique. The central pull-out test is an ideal way of checking that each technique has been fully understood.

As the CEM exam is not pinned down to a set of question types, it is especially important for a child to have solid knowledge that can be used in a variety of ways. The skills in this book are presented in different formats and the assessment papers that go with this book provide additional practice at each level.

How is this book organised?

The questions here have been organised under Comprehension, Vocabulary, Cloze tests and Mixed grammar to cover each of the question types in a logical order. Each section is labelled to match the tutorial links which can be found throughout the *Bond CEM English and Verbal Reasoning Assessment Papers* to give a clear structure to both this book and the assessment papers. Each question type is introduced and a worked example is given, followed by questions for your child to work through to ensure there is a thorough understanding of each question type. There are many examples of each question style for a child to try with a clear progression through the book based on understanding techniques before moving on to the next section. In the assessment papers, these individual skills are mixed throughout each paper to replicate an exam. This is an excellent way of consolidating skills as they are understood and recalled in each paper. If a child is struggling with the assessment papers, it is easy to then refer back to this book for further consolidation of any tricky areas.

In the centre of the book there is then a full examination paper testing each of the question types covered in the book. This book also includes a 'How do you prepare for the exam?' section, to help with the actual exam itself, how to deal with timing issues and how to deal with questions that your child may have never seen. This is followed by a glossary containing key terms and an answer section so that you can see how you would have scored. Finally, there is a resources section with books and free online materials that will help to support your child.

Checklist

What do you need to use with this book?

✔ A ready supply of **pencils** and **erasers**

✔ A pad of **paper** for working out

✔ A **dictionary** and **thesaurus** to keep close to hand

✔ A quiet, **well-lit area** in which to work

✔ You may want to see *Focus on Comprehension* for further comprehension help

---

 PARENT TIP

Your exam might be standard format – this is where a pupil writes the answer on a line or it might be in multiple-choice format – this is where a pupil has a choice of answers to select from. If a child can complete a standard format paper, then a multiple-choice paper is advantageous. If, however, your child only completes multiple-choice papers, a standard format will be significantly harder, so make sure that your child feels secure with all of these question types and can then practise their newfound skills with the CEM English and Verbal Reasoning Assessment Papers.

Parent tips and information

When should you start using this book?

The Parents' Guide to the 11⁺ is a great resource for assessing your child and for creating your own learning plan. This will suggest the best time to begin with an 11⁺ programme, but whether your child has a year or a month before the exam, this book should prove useful. If you have sufficient time before the exam, you may want to use this book to support school work, as the comprehension, vocabulary and mixed grammar sections will underpin the school curriculum.

What else can I do to support my child through the 11⁺?

The 11⁺ process should be a fun journey of extending your child's love of learning, which they begin from the moment they are born. A love of words, of reading, of solving problems and thinking logically are such important skills that it is never too late, nor too early to begin this process. In general, the best advice is to encourage your child to do well at school with their school homework. Ensure that your child knows their times tables, that they learn their spellings and that they get into a regular, effective reading habit.

Although it is wonderful to give your child the experience of museums, galleries, cultural events and travel, much effective learning costs very little. Activities such as baking, hobbies, gardening, word searches, puzzles, reading, creating stories, making 'newspapers' – all of these can teach valuable skills about measurements, scientific processes, problem solving, vocabulary building, logical reasoning and creativity. A balance of activities on a regular basis is far more productive than an occasional event.

Building strong foundation skills as a part of everyday life is so important and much of this can be informal. For example, take your child into a greengrocer's or supermarket and show them the wide range of fruit and vegetables by name, type, taste, country of origin and so on. Look at paint samples and discuss colours so that your child knows that lilac and violet are purple and navy and azure are blue.

In terms of extending English and verbal reasoning, the following are some ideas that you can take on board to help your child to develop knowledge and skills.

- Read to your child, asking questions such as 'What do you think will happen next?' and 'How do you think that character feels?' This will help with comprehension skills.
- Set a good example by reading in front of your child and discussing what you have read. Let them see that reading is an integral part of life – everything from reading charts and tables on food labels or train timetables, to reading novels on the beach or newspapers around the table.
- Listen to your child reading and ask them what they like or dislike about what they have read.
- Play with words by choosing a new word a day for the family to use or through games like Scrabble®, Scattergories® or Boggle®.

- Use a dictionary and a thesaurus on a regular basis so that your child learns to look up words they do not know or find alternative words.
- Encourage your child to write on a regular basis, perhaps by keeping a journal or writing stories and poems – anything that they enjoy and that can extend their vocabulary.
- Join the local library and make this a regular treat.
- Encourage your child to read picture books to younger siblings and to consolidate useful general knowledge, such as the names of baby animals or the months of the year.

 PARENT TIP

Don't underestimate the power of 'fun' learning: watching quiz programmes on television, watching science and discovery programmes, taking part in quizzes and playing the type of board games that help with both extending vocabulary and general knowledge.

READING ROUTINES

From the earliest age, you can help your child to foster a love of reading by making it a fun activity. Read to your child, talk about words, encourage games like 'I spy' or 'find a word that rhymes with…' and remember that children love repetition. However boring it might be to us, children do like to have their favourite stories repeatedly retold and this is a vital stage in their learning and in setting up their love of reading. The single most important thing you can do at this age is to begin a reading routine – last thing at night or first thing in the morning is a good idea as these times can be easier to maintain. Allow your child to pick the story that they want you to read.

By the age of eight or nine, children should be able to read fluently, but they will still love listening to stories. Try audiobooks in addition to reading to children. In your reading routine, try reading a paragraph each with your child or read to them for half of the reading time and let them read alone for half of the time. It doesn't matter if this is the same book or a different book. The aim is to eventually reach a point when your child reads independently, but this doesn't mean that you should stop reading to your child.

If you are unable to read to your child, for whatever reason, audiobooks are an excellent substitute and your library should have a range to choose from. The aim is to get a reading habit in place and to develop a real love of reading. It is incredibly difficult to try to get a teenager to read if they have never had a reading routine.

My child hates reading – what do I do?

Try to find out why your child hates reading. Have they got a book that is too challenging? Do they find reading difficult? Are they too tired to read? Are they too energetic to read? It is worth looking at several things that might have an impact upon your child, such as:

- Does your child have a reading issue? Check with your child's school teacher to ensure that there is no reading or word difficulty.
- Check that the book your child is reading is not too difficult or too easy.
- Try to find a book that suits your child's interests. A factual book on football or a hobby may suit your child better than fiction and this is fine if your child prefers it.
- A wide range of reading material offers the best learning experience for your child, so don't restrict reading to just a night-time routine. Consider a children's newspaper for the weekend, factual books for researching a topic or hobby, fiction for car journeys or comics for an after-school treat.
- If you are establishing a night-time reading routine, ensure that your child has preparation for it. If you tell them to turn the television off or stop playing a favourite game to read, they will associate reading as negative and something that stops their fun. Make sure that before reading, children are not too tired and have already stopped their activities.
- Make sure that reading is a positive experience for your child. Do they have sufficient light to read? Is the book they are reading comfortable to hold? Does your child prefer a paper book or an electronic format? Do you talk positively about reading? Does your child see that you enjoy reading and that it isn't just 'something the school wants'?
- Let your child choose at least some of the books that they want to read. Ask the librarian for their recommendation of suitable books based on your child's interests or favourite authors.
- If your child is 'addicted' to one author, it is better to read anything than to read nothing so encourage this, but perhaps try to find other authors that are similar or who write about similar topics and themes. Encourage a broad spectrum of authors – insisting that your child only reads classic literature may dampen the best young reader's enthusiasm!

Comprehension

The key areas in Comprehension are:

- spotting
- inference and deduction
- vocabulary
- text types
- spelling rules
- literary effects.

'Comprehension is to just read the text and to answer questions on it.' Easy! Well not always. Some of the question types can be tricky to solve for the full amount of marks and many children manage to answer the questions but drop a significant number of marks. Difficulties can arise in understanding what the question is looking for and in not answering specifically enough to gain full marks. Here are the key areas of comprehension and as each area requires a specific skill, we'll look at each one in turn and explore how pupils can develop the skills needed.

(A) Spotting

Many comprehension questions require close and clever reading to spot information. This might be finding names, places or other key words and we can use two useful strategies to do this. When first reading a comprehension text, you need to read carefully and with full concentration to gain maximum information first time through. Some children find it easier to underline key words such as names, dates and places or to write short notes at the side of the text such as 'Grandma's house', 'my house' or 'school' to help them find the information again quickly. The other skill needed is to then speed-read to find information quickly to answer the questions. If you have read the text properly with close reading, then skimming is just to look for the key words in order to move through the text quickly and effectively. Here is an example text with a typical spotting question:

'Michael eagerly opened his *Death-defying Dangerous Dinosaurs* book and marvelled at the illustrations. He loved this book and his favourite dinosaur was the Tyrannosaurus rex.'

Q. Which dinosaur did Michael like best?

Michael liked the Tyrannosaurus best.

Here is an example text with some spotting questions to try:

Now it's your turn!

Mrs Crockett had owned the toy shop for over 30 years. Generations of young children had come into the shop and had gazed at the fashion of the day: from racing cars to talking dolls, big, fat teddy bears to board games and craft kits. Mrs Crockett had always thought that her children would take on the business, but Jack, who had always loved his toy animals, worked at the zoo and Millie, who had spent all of her time combing her dolls' hair, was a hairdresser with her own salon. Now that Mrs Crockett was close to retirement, she did wonder who would take on her beloved shop.

1 How long has Mrs Crockett owned the toy shop? (1)

_____

2 What was Mrs Crockett's daughter called? (1)

_____

3 What job did Mrs Crockett's son do? (1)

_____

4 Who liked to comb her dolls' hair? (1)

   a Mrs Crockett

   b Jack

   c Millie

5 What were the teddy bears in the shop like? (1)

   a long and fluffy

   b big and fat

   c cuddly and squashy

6 What job did Mrs Crockett's daughter do? (1)

   a She works at the toy shop

   b She works at a zoo

   c She owns a hairdressing salon

REMEMBER!

Imagine that you asked someone what their name was and they answered with their name, address, date of birth, favourite pet and what colour their bedroom was painted. You would think this strange, wouldn't you? Well comprehension is the same. You don't need to copy a whole sentence to prove your point as your answer will be incorrect. Remember to be precise.

B Inference and deduction

These two skills are really important in comprehension. Inference is to look at evidence and to guess what might have happened. Deduction is to look at evidence and to know what has happened. To build these skills, you need to look carefully at what happens in the text and to keep asking yourself, 'What is happening? Why is it happening? How do I know this?' Here is an example text with a typical inference and a typical deduction question:

'Michael eagerly opened his *Death-defying Dangerous Dinosaurs* book and marvelled at the illustrations. He loved this book and his favourite dinosaur was the Tyrannosaurus rex.'

Q. Do you think that Michael likes reading?

Yes, I think that Michael likes reading because he loved this particular book and he was eager to open the book, so there are other books that Michael probably likes.

Q. Does Michael like dinosaurs? Find evidence to support your view.

Yes, Michael likes dinosaurs because the text says that his favourite dinosaur was the Tyrannosaurus rex.

With inference, we know that Michael likes to read this book so we can logically follow this through and assume that Michael is likely to enjoy reading. We don't know this, but we have clues in the text that would suggest that he does enjoy reading.

With deduction, we have more evidence because we know that Michael's favourite book is about dinosaurs and he has a specific dinosaur that he likes best of all.

To recap: Look for words, emotions, information and clues, and if there is sufficient evidence to be secure, you can make your deduction. If the evidence is less secure but you still have some clues that lead you to your response, then you can make an inference.

Here is another piece of text with some questions so see how you do. Remember, you are a spy looking for every single clue.

Captain Portman looked in the mirror at his reflection. His smart uniform with polished gold buttons looked impressive enough, but the range of medals, stripes, ribbons and pips told another story. There was nothing smart and polished in the trenches filled with mud, blood and driving rain. There was nothing impressive about killing other people in order to save your own people. Captain Portman's carefully combed moustache stood to attention and not a hair was out of place in his sharply brushed back hair. Now he could fashion his hair, his moustache, his black shiny shoes, but if only his family knew what he looked like after weeks on end standing in water until the skin on his feet and legs blistered and rotted. No, Captain Portman didn't want anyone to have to hear about the horrors that he had seen. Pushing back the tears that never felt far away, he bit his lip and focused at the face in the mirror. He was just 17 when he joined and within 36 hours he had aged by decades. How did he get through those years? But today was for family. Today was for celebration.

Q. Captain Portman is a proud man. Do you agree with this? Use the text to support your view. (3)

_____

_____

_____

_____

_____

_____

Q. Captain Portman is a happy man. Do you agree with this? Use the text to support your view. (3)

_____

_____

_____

_____

_____

_____

Q. Did Captain Portman enjoy being 18? Use the text to support your view. (3)

_____

_____

_____

_____

_____

_____

> Q. Is Captain Portman close to his family? Use the text to support
>   your view.   (3)
>
> _____
>
> _____
>
> _____
>
> _____
>
> _____
>
> _____

How did you do with these questions? Here are some suggested responses to compare to yours:

Q. Captain Portman is a proud man. Do you agree with this? Use the text to support your view.

I do not think that Captain Portman is a proud man. Captain Portman takes pride in his appearance. His buttons are polished, his hair is smart and his moustache is 'carefully combed'. However, the text refers to the war as being 'nothing smart' and 'nothing impressive' so I think he feels relieved to be out of the war, but not proud of what he had to do.

Q. Captain Portman is a happy man. Do you agree with this? Use the text to support your view.

I do not think that Captain Portman is a happy man. The text states that he is never far from tears and he cannot share his horrific experiences with other people. I think he is lonely, shocked, has seen things and had to do things that are truly horrendous and the fact that he is always 'pushing back the tears' shows his sadness.

Q. Did Captain Portman enjoy being 18? Use the text to support your view.

I do not think that Captain Portman enjoyed being 18 because the text states that he joined the war at 17 and he had to get through 'years'. This tells us that he was in the war while he was 18 and this would not be a time of enjoyment as he has already expressed the horror he had seen. The text refers to him having 'aged by decades' in less than three days.

Q. Is Captain Portman close to his family? Use the text to support your view.

Captain Portman is close enough to want to make the effort in his appearance and dress. He is also prepared to fight back the tears and to protect his family from what he has witnessed and experienced. He wishes at times that 'if only his family knew' as he wants them to understand and to share his burden, but he knows that he has to protect them.

Did you find the same clues as I did? Were you able to use deduction and inference to work out your response and to use these clues to support your view?

Here is another example text with some inference and deduction questions to try:

REMEMBER!

The more you practise this skill, the easier it will be for you so now is the time to read some crime books and see if you can solve the problem before the detectives. Become curious and ask 'Why did the character do that?' or 'What is the significance of that?' and you will be well on your way to being a successful comprehension spy!

Now it's your turn!

Mrs Crockett had owned the toy shop for over thirty years. Generations of young children had come into the shop and had gazed at the fashion of the day: from racing cars to talking dolls, big, fat teddy bears to board games and craft kits. Mrs Crockett had always thought that her children would take on the business, but Jack, who had always loved his toy animals, worked at the zoo and Millie, who had spent all of her time combing her dolls' hair, was a hairdresser with her own salon. Now that Mrs Crockett was close to retirement she did wonder who would take on her beloved shop.

7 'Mrs Crockett is a young woman.' Do you agree with this statement? Find two pieces of evidence to support your view. (3)

_____

_____

_____

_____

8 What does Mrs Crockett think about her shop? Use the text to support your answer. (2)

_____

_____

_____

_____

9 From reading the text, do you think that toys can influence the career that children have when they grow up? (2)

_____

_____

_____

_____

_____

10 Are the same toys popular every year? Use the text to support your answer. (2)

_____

_____

_____

_____

11 'Technology makes toys popular.' Do you agree with this statement? Find two pieces of evidence to support your view. (1)

_____

_____

_____

_____

REMEMBER!

Have you noticed that some questions only score 1 mark each while others have more marks available? As a rule of thumb, there is usually one mark per piece of evidence or response, so do check that your answer has enough information to score the maximum number of marks. Likewise, if a question only has 1 mark, it only requires a quick answer.

If your child struggles with spotting, inference and deduction, try to encourage this type of analytical thinking. Here are some ideas that can really help with this:

- *If someone is laughing, ask your child why they might be laughing? What types of things make people laugh? Look for clues – is something funny on the television? Are they listening to a joke? Is someone tickling them? You might need to prompt them initially but if they are okay with this, try the same approach with someone who is angry, crying, sleepy or frightened.*
- *Try looking at some riddles with your child where they need to consider a range of clues to find a solution.*
- *Consider games like Cluedo or strategy games where inference, spotting and recall are important in the game.*
- *When your child is reading, ask them questions about what they have read. Try to encourage more critical thinking by asking them to predict what will happen next and why they think this. What clues are there to predict action? What are the characters like and how might their nature be important in their book? A way of formalising this is to help your child create 'Top Trump' type cards using the major characters. Grade them by personality traits and perhaps consider how the book might change if a certain character was not there or if they had a different characteristic.*

Ⓒ *Vocabulary*

Building vocabulary is a really useful skill for many question types. In comprehension, a good vocabulary is important as you will often be asked to explain what words mean as used in the text. This means not only knowing a word, but also knowing how it might be used in context. Context is also useful as a clue for what a word might mean, so make sure that you look carefully at the sentence to find the answer. Here is an example text with a typical vocabulary question and possible answers:

'Michael eagerly opened his *Death-defying Dangerous Dinosaurs* book and marvelled at the illustrations. He loved this book and his favourite dinosaur was the Tyrannosaurus rex.'

Q. What do these words mean as used in the text?

   a eagerly   *enthusiastically, keenly, excitedly*

   b marvelled   *wondered, admired, appreciated*

   c illustrations *pictures, drawings*

Can you see that there are several words that would work? Any one of these answers would gain a mark. It is also important to get the right ending of the word. 'Eagerly' is an adverb, which describes how something is done, so the answer must also be an adverb. For example, it would not be 'keen', but 'keenly'. Here is another example text with some vocabulary questions to try:

Now it's your turn!

Mrs Crockett had owned the toy shop for over thirty years. Generations of young children had come into the shop and had gazed at the fashion of the day: from racing cars to talking dolls, big, fat teddy bears to board games and craft kits. Mrs Crockett had always thought that her children would take on the business, but Jack, who had always loved his toy animals, worked at the zoo and Millie, who had spent all of her time combing her dolls' hair, was a hairdresser with her own salon. Now that Mrs Crockett was close to retirement, she did wonder who would take on her beloved shop.

12 What do these words mean as used in the text? (3)

    a gazed _____

    b wonder _____

    c beloved _____

13 Which word is used in the text to mean the following? (3)

    a over a long period of time _____

    b the latest must-have _____

    c getting near _____

✔ PARENT TIP

Showing your child how to use a dictionary and a thesaurus will give them a really useful skill. A quick game that you can play with a dictionary is to name a letter of the alphabet and encourage your child to find the words beginning with that letter as quickly as possible. The more accurate your child can be, the quicker he or she will be able to use a dictionary in everyday life.

☀ REMEMBER!

Why not make your own 'personal dictionary'? Copy down any unknown words that you come across in your book. Check in the dictionary or ask someone what the word means and you can write down the definition. Keep your book close to you when you are reading and add words whenever you can.

(D) Text types

Knowing the common elements of each text type helps you to answer these questions. Here is a quick reminder of the top five points for each text type:

A letter

Checklist

- ✔ A letter has an address at the top of the page.
- ✔ A letter has a date underneath the address.
- ✔ A letter may be formal or informal.
- ✔ A letter begins with words such as 'Dear _____' or 'Hi'.
- ✔ A letter ends with words such as 'Yours Sincerely' or 'Love from'.

A story

Checklist

✓ A story is written in prose with the text divided into paragraphs.

✓ A story is written in chapters.

✓ A story is usually written in the third person with characters referred to by name.

✓ A story has a plot.

✓ A story uses descriptive language.

A play script

Checklist

✓ The characters' names are written in the left-hand margin of the page.

✓ A play script is written in dialogue (speech).

✓ A play script does not use speech marks.

✓ A play script is written in acts and scenes to divide the text.

✓ Stage directions are given in brackets.

A poem

Checklist

✓ A poem has short lines.

✓ A poem is often divided into short stanzas.

✓ Each line usually begins with a capital letter.

✓ Not all lines have to end with a full stop or any other punctuation.

✓ A poem uses imaginative words with metaphors, personification or other literary effects.

A website page

Checklist

✓ A website might have a 'www' address.

✓ A website is often written in columns or with 'buttons' to jump to other pages.

✓ A website may use diagrams and charts.

✓ A website uses factual, informative writing.

✓ A website may use bullet points and hyperlinks.

A newspaper or magazine article

Checklist

- ✓ A newspaper or magazine article will use titles and subtitles.
- ✓ A newspaper or magazine article will be written in columns.
- ✓ A newspaper or magazine article often uses facts and figures.
- ✓ A newspaper or magazine article might use diagrams, charts, photos, pictures or graphics.
- ✓ A newspaper or magazine article is usually factual, informative writing.

Reports or accounts

Checklist

- ✓ A report or account uses factual, informative writing.
- ✓ A report or account is usually written in the first person using the word 'I'.
- ✓ A report or account may use statistics and numbers.
- ✓ A report or account uses formal language.
- ✓ A report or account might use titles, subtitles and bullet points to divide the text.

A recipe or set of instructions

Checklist

- ✓ A recipe or set of instructions uses informative writing.
- ✓ A recipe or set of instructions is broken into clearly defined steps, usually numbered.
- ✓ A recipe or set of instructions might use diagrams or pictures to help explain stages.
- ✓ A recipe or set of instructions may use headings, subheadings and bullet points.
- ✓ A recipe or set of instructions uses as few words as is necessary to get a point across.

A typical text type question might be, 'What type of text do you think this is? Find three pieces of evidence to support your view.' By remembering the top points for each of these text types, it will be easier to recognise what the text type is and to find proof that will support your answer.

 **PARENT TIP**

Encourage your child to read a play, a poem, a letter, a recipe, an invoice, a bank statement, an instruction manual, the back of a cereal box – anything that allows a child to recognise a wide range of text types and writing styles.

Here is an example text with a text type question to try:

Now it's your turn!

Mrs Crockett had owned the toy shop for over 30 years. Generations of young children had come into the shop and had gazed at the fashion of the day: from racing cars to talking dolls, big, fat teddy bears to board games and craft kits. Mrs Crockett had always thought that her children would take on the business, but Jack, who had always loved his toy animals, worked at the zoo and Millie, who had spent all of her time combing her dolls' hair, was a hairdresser with her own salon. Now that Mrs Crockett was close to retirement, she did wonder who would take on her beloved shop.

14 What type of text do you think this extract is taken from? Find three pieces of evidence to support your answer. (4)

_____

_____

_____

_____

_____

_____

E Spelling rules

Spelling rules are so important, not only for getting spellings correct, but also for recognising root words, suffixes and prefixes. Remember that a root word is the main part of a word, a prefix is a group of letters added to the beginning of a root and a suffix is a group of letters that are added to the end of a word. Sometimes the root word needs to change its spelling before the suffix is added.

Here are some of the most common spelling rules with some examples that follow the rule and some examples of words that are exceptions to the rule:

'i before e except after c':

fierce, pierce, diet, receive, ceiling, receipt
words that don't fit the rule: weight, height, weird

Before adding a suffix, double the last consonant if it is single and follows a single vowel:

run + ing = running
knit + er = knitter
recap + ing = recapping

If the word has an 'f' turn it into a 've' before adding the plural ending:

scarf = scarves
knife = knives
calf = calves

If a word ends in 'ch', 'sh' or 'x', the plural ending is 'es':

church = churches
wish = wishes
box = boxes

If the word ends in 'y', take off the 'y' and add 'ies' for the plural except if a word ends in 'key':

baby = babies
puppy = puppies,
monkey = monkeys

PARENT TIP

See the Mixed grammar section for more information on single and plural words and on roots, prefixes and suffixes.

Some words sound the same as another word but have a different meaning and a different spelling. These words are called homophones. Here are some examples of homophones:

to/too/two
their/there/they're
which/witch
red/read
weather/whether
pair/pear/pare

PARENT TIP

See section 3D Contextual words, for more information on homophones.

Here is an example text with a typical vocabulary question:

'Michael eagerly opened his *Death-defying Dangerous Dinosaurs* book and marvelled at the illustrations. He loved this book and his favourite dinosaur was the Tyrannosaurus rex.'

Q. The word 'open' has become 'opened'. Why is this?

The word 'opened' is in the past tense so we have to add the suffix 'ed'.

Q. Find another word in the extract that has the same spelling rule.

The word 'love' has become 'loved'.

Here is an example text with some spelling rule questions for you to try:

Now it's your turn!

Mrs Crockett had owned the toy shop for over 30 years. Generations of young children had come into the shop and had gazed at the fashion of the day: from racing cars to talking dolls, big, fat teddy bears to board games and craft kits. Mrs Crockett had always thought that her children would take on the business, but Jack, who had always loved his toy animals, worked at the zoo and Millie, who had spent all of her time combing her dolls' hair, was a hairdresser with her own salon. Now that Mrs Crockett was close to retirement, she did wonder who would take on her beloved shop.

15 The word 'talk' has become 'talking'. Why is this? (1)

_____

_____

_____

16 Can you find another word in the extract that follows the same rule? (1)

_____

17 The word 'do' has become 'did'. Why is this? (1)

_____

_____

_____

18 Can you find another word in the extract that follows the same rule? (1)

_____

19 Can you find a homophone in the first sentence of the extract? (1)

_____

20 Can you change these plural words to singular? (3)

    a generations _____

    b children _____

    c dolls _____

21 Can you change these single words into plurals? (3)

    a business _____

    b zoo _____

    c hairdresser _____

REMEMBER!

Make sure that you know your school spellings and revise spelling rules to help you recognise how and why a word has been used.

(F) Literary effects

Literary effects or literary devices are techniques that writers use to create interest in their writing. Here are some of the most common ones that you will need to recognise:

Alliteration: This is when words have the same starting sound such as 'Caitlin's clever cat'.

Irony: This is when a word is described as being the opposite of its real state. For example, describing a very tall person called Len as 'Little Len' would be ironic because someone very tall is not little. Another example might be referring to a 'minor mishap' when in reality the whole house has burnt down, all possessions have gone and there is nothing left standing. It would be ironic because an awful disaster as serious as this could never be called 'minor' or a 'mishap'.

Listing: This is where words are placed in a list to draw attention to them. For example, 'I went shopping, visiting, watching and waiting' or 'She was tall, slim, pale and sad.'

Metaphor: This is when something is described as actually being something else, rather than like something else. For example, 'my hands are ice' (not 'my hands are as cold as ice') or 'cruel arrows shot from my mouth' (not 'words as cruel as arrows shot from my mouth').

Onomatopoeia: This is where a word imitates the sound or action that it is describing, for example, 'bang', 'pop' or 'crash'.

Personification: This is where we describe something that is not human, as having human qualities, for example, 'the angry sky' or 'my blanket hugged me' or 'even the sun hid its face from me'.

Repetition: This is where a word or phrase is repeated for effect, such as 'no worry, no stress, no cost, no problem' or 'it was a long, long, long time ago'.

Simile: This is when we describe something as being 'like' something else or 'as' something else. For example, 'I am as cold as ice' or 'my hands are like blocks of ice'.

Symbolism: This is where something trivial represents something really important, such as a young girl building a snowman with the new next-door neighbour's boy. She later marries the neighbour's boy and whenever she sees a snowman, she automatically thinks of her husband. Another example might be a child who eats a jam sandwich and is violently sick shortly afterwards, then every time they see a jam sandwich, they feel very sick.

Here is an example text with a typical literary effect question:

> 'Michael eagerly opened his *Death-defying Dangerous Dinosaurs* book and marvelled at the illustrations. He loved this book and his favourite dinosaur was the Tyrannosaurus rex.'
>
> **Q. Can you find an example of alliteration in this extract?**
>
> *The phrase 'death-defying dangerous dinosaurs' is an example of alliteration.*

Here is an example text with some literary effects questions for you to try:

Now it's your turn!

Mrs Crockett had owned the toy shop for over 30 years. Generations of young children had come into the shop and had gazed at the fashion of the day: from racing cars to talking dolls, big, fat teddy bears to board games and craft kits. Mrs Crockett had always thought that her children would take on the business, but Jack, who had always loved his toy animals, worked at the zoo and Millie, who had spent all of her time combing her dolls' hair, was a hairdresser with her own salon. Now that Mrs Crockett was close to retirement, she did wonder who would take on her beloved shop.

22 How do Jack's toy animals become important or 'symbolic'? (2)

_____

_____

_____

_____

23 The author uses lists of toys in the extract. What effect does this create? (1)

_____

_____

_____

_____

Now that we've looked at a range of comprehension questions, here is a quick recap:

 PARENT TIP

The Bond range of comprehension books can help provide a wider range of comprehension exercises to work through. Focus on Comprehension _is a useful book to explain comprehension in more detail._

How Did You Do?

In this section there were 40 marks available in the 'Now it's your turn' exercises. Check your answers against the list on page 96. How many did you score?

- 34 or fewer correct? Work through the question types again and make sure that you fully understand each section. Once you have done this, try the questions again before you move on.
- 35 correct or more. Well done! Do check any questions that were incorrect and make sure you understand where you made mistakes and why. Here is a comprehension test with a mixture of question types for you to try.

Comprehension test

Read the following text and then answer the questions that follow.

www.Eyesightedsite.co.uk www.Eyesightedsite.co.uk www.Eyesightedsite.co.uk

HOME   ABOUT   GALLERY

Dispensing Opticians	Optometrists
A dispensing optician has to go through a period of academic study plus practical experience before he or she is qualified.	An optometrist studies for even longer and also has a period of practical experience before he or she is qualified.
Dispensing opticians can provide professional advice on all manner of glasses from night driving lenses, sunglasses and safety eyewear through to sports glasses and advice on contact lenses.	An optometrist is the person qualified to examine eyes, use a variety of sight tests and prescribe glasses or contact lenses for anyone who needs them.
A dispensing optician has a responsible job in helping the optometrist provide the best possible eye care for everyone.	Optometrists can provide help and advice on all manner of visual problems and can spot eye diseases, disorders or sight issues, prescribing treatments when necessary or referring patients to doctors or other medical specialists before they become more serious.

Common Children's Eye Problems	How to Help Children's Eyesight
Some eye problems that are especially common in children include a 'lazy eye', properly called amblyopia. This is where one eye will not work as it should as the child's brain will not accept vision through both eyes, meaning that the vision in the weak eye refuses to develop fully. Fortunately, this can be corrected easily by forcing the weaker eye to recover through covering the strong eye, along with sight therapy to train this weaker eye to work. In many cases, the younger the child is when they begin treatment, the more successful and quicker the treatment is.	To help develop a child's eyesight, toys should be placed 20–30 cm away from the child. Hanging a mobile above a baby's cot and providing toys for a baby to look at and to focus on will help. Encouraging a baby to crawl while talking means that the baby uses its eyes to follow you, and helps a child to develop good eyesight. As the child grows older, activities that improve motor and hand-to-eye coordination are recommended. Activities such as building blocks, puzzles, pegboards, drawing and painting are all ideal activities. Providing sun protection through a sun hat or sunglasses will help to protect a child's eyes, as will providing proper protective eyewear.

Click here to see our gallery where we have the very latest in all eyewear, including safety glasses, sunglasses, reading glasses, every day glasses, special occasion glasses and spectacle fashion accessories such as our best-selling glasses holders and a wide range of fashionable glasses cases. Your eyes are windows to the soul, so they deserve the very best.

1 What five things can dispensing opticians offer as part of their advice?

_____

_____

_____

_____

_____

_____ ◯ 5

2 What seven things can an optometrist do?

_____

_____

_____

_____

_____

_____ ◯ 7

3 How can an eye-patch help with amblyopia?

_____

_____

_____ ◯ 1

4 How does encouraging a baby to crawl help their eyesight?

_____

_____

_____ ◯ 1

5 Would making models out of clay help a child's sight development or not?
Use the text to support your answer.

_____

_____

_____ ◯ 2

6 'There is no point going to an optician unless you have got a problem.'
Would you agree with this or not? Find three pieces of evidence to support
your answer.

_____

_____

_____

_____ ◯ 4

7 What do these words mean as used in the text?

a variety _____

b corrected _____

c occasion _____ ◯ 3

8 Which word is used in the text to mean the following:

a a page of photographs and pictures: _____

b familiarity and repetition of doing a job: _____

c difficult or troublesome: _____ ◯ 3

9 What type of text do you think this extract is from? Find four pieces of
evidence to support your answer.

_____

_____

_____

_____

_____

_____ ◯ 5

10 The word 'activity' has been written as 'activities'.

a Why is this? _____

_____

b Can you find another word in the extract that has the same spelling rule?

_____ ◯ 2

11 The word 'provide' is written as 'providing'.

   a What spelling rule has been applied?

_____

   b Can you find another word that has the same spelling rule?

_____ ◯ 2

12 Can you find a metaphor in the last paragraph?

_____ ◯ 1

13 In the 'How To Help Children's Eyesight' section, can you find an example of alliteration?

_____ ◯ 1

💡 REMEMBER!

If you have found any of these questions tricky, reread the section based on the question type and make sure that you understand it. The answer section at the end of this book also makes it clear how the answer has been found so check that the answer makes sense to you. If this is still tricky, try looking at *Bond 11⁺ English* or *Bond Focus on Comprehension* to help with specific techniques.

2 Vocabulary

The key areas in vocabulary are:

- synonyms grid
- antonyms grid
- words most similar
- words most opposite
- words matching pairs of words
- odd words out
- logical reasoning.

Vocabulary looks at words and their meanings. Many of these question types can be tricky as it requires skills in knowing a word and how many definitions there might be of that word. It requires close reading skills and the ability to gain maximum information from every word. Vocabulary also requires children to work out words that might be similar or opposite to another word. Each area requires a specific skill, so we'll look at each one and at how you can develop the skills needed to solve vocabulary questions.

(A) Synonyms grid

(B) Antonyms grid

This question type offers a grid of words from which you can choose to answer the synonym and antonym questions. Here is a typical synonym and antonym grid question:

large	weaken	valuable	night	sore
cramped	agile	stick	bright	vast
adhere	remember	restricted	silly	welcome
memorable	confined	huge	fine	glut
foolish	worthless	forceful	flexible	ached

Q. Find three synonyms for the word 'big'.

large, huge, vast

Q. Find three antonyms for the word 'spacious'.

cramped, confined, restricted

Q. Find two synonyms for the word 'glue'.

adhere, stick

Q. Find two antonyms for the word 'rigid'.

agile, flexible

The key to these question types is to understand that a synonym is a word with a similar meaning and an antonym is a word with an opposite meaning. As these questions can be worth a lot of marks, they are worth solving well, so here are some useful techniques to help:

Synonym questions

1 Look at the word that is being matched and scan the grid for words that are most similar to this word.
2 Once you have found a word, place a neat line through it.
3 Continue until you have found all of the words required.

REMEMBER!

Begin with the synonyms and then look at the antonyms so that you can lessen the number of words to consider as you go along. It is also worth rejecting any words you find in the box that you know do not have an opposite, leaving even fewer words to choose from!

Antonym questions

1 Look at the grid and place a neat line through all of the words that you know cannot have an opposite, but don't reject any words unless you are certain. For example, the word 'cat' does not have an opposite, but the word 'queen' may have 'king' as an opposite (a queen is a female royal ruler), or it may have 'tom' as an opposite (a female cat is called a queen).
2 Now look at the word that you need to find an opposite for, and ask yourself what an opposite might be. For example, if I am finding the antonym for 'good' I might think bad, awful, naughty and rotten.
3 Now scan the grid and you will hopefully find the words that you are looking for.

Looking for words when you don't know the meaning of them

It is always tricky if the word that you are trying to find a synonym or antonym for is unknown to you, or if you find a word in the grid that you don't know. Here are two techniques that might help:

Context knowledge
- If you don't know a word, think about whether you have ever heard of it in any context before. If so, when or how did you hear about it?
- This might help you find another word that is also connected.
- For example, if you don't know the word 'valuable', you might have heard the phrase 'Keep your valuables close to you or in the safe.'
- You know that you would use a safe to store money, jewellery or important documents, so words such as 'priceless', 'costly' or 'treasured' might all be associated with 'valuable'.

Remember that the word 'context' just means how the word fits in with other words around it. Think about the word 'bright'. What does it mean? Now look at the word 'bright' in the sentences below and think about what it means:

The child was clearly bright and always scored top marks in exams.
The weather was so bright and sunny last week that we went on a picnic.
I love those bright red shoes as they look great with that dress.

Now does context make more sense?

Root word knowledge

- Have you got a root word that you might recognise?
- For example, you may not know the word 'disproportionate' but do you know the root? Let's take away the 'dis' prefix to make 'proportionate'. Now let's take away the 'ate' suffix to make 'proportion'.
- Now, you probably know that drawing something in proportion means that you shouldn't draw a huge head on a tiny body or a tiny head on a huge body. Everything must fit together in size.
- You may also know that the 'dis' prefix means 'not' or 'opposite of'.
- Perhaps then the word 'disproportionate' means 'not in proportion'.

 PARENT TIP

A working knowledge of your prefixes and suffixes can be useful in these word grids so look at the Mixed grammar section for more on this.

Here are some typical synonym and antonym questions to try:

Now it's your turn!

Look at the following words and then use them to answer the questions that follow.

base	night	dawn	moon	calm
noon	bottom	remember	disorganised	closed
mild	sunrise	stars	mare	finger
messy	clear	mayor	transparent	sunset
dusk	unopened	toe	sun	nail

1 Find two synonyms for the word 'evening'. (2)

_____

2 Find two antonyms for the word 'opaque'.　(2)

_____

3 Find two synonyms for the word 'gentle'.　(2)

_____

4 Find two antonyms for the word 'neat'.　(2)

_____

spin	trot	pause	frail	grind
stamp	deceive	entrance	giggle	store
strong	tissue	cry	cheat	roam
envelope	laugh	trick	rest	keep
staple	paper	turn	entry	robust

5 Find two synonyms for the word 'betray'.　(2)

_____

6 Find two antonyms for the word 'exit'.　(2)

_____

7 Find two synonyms for the word 'rotate'.　(2)

_____

8 Find two antonyms for the word 'continue'.　(2)

_____

REMEMBER!

Here's a quick way to remember the meaning of synonyms and antonyms: if synonyms mean similar words, then antonyms must be opposites.

Antonym and synonym questions are really testing your vocabulary and knowledge of the definition of words and how they can be used. Reading a wide range of material is a good way of building vocabulary, but puzzles, general knowledge books, vocabulary books and spelling books are all excellent ways of extending your knowledge.

(C) *Words most similar*

(D) *Words most opposite*

The antonyms and synonyms in the word grid cover one type of vocabulary question. Here are some other popular formats that use antonyms and synonyms:

Q. **Underline the one word on the right that is most opposite to the word on the left.**

frail   weak / dainty / <u>robust</u> / hot / heavy

Q. **Underline the one word on the right that is most similar to the word on the left.**

frail   <u>weak</u> / dainty / robust / hot / heavy

Q. **Add the missing letters to the word on the right to make a word with opposite meaning to the word on the left.**

frail   r _ _ u _ t

frail   *r o b u s t*

Q. **Add the missing letters to the word on the right to make a word with similar meaning to the word on the left.**

frail   w _ _ k

frail   *w e a k*

With all of these question formats, it is word knowledge that you need to have, but there are limited options to choose from. Let's look at a technique to help solve these question types:

Q. **Underline the one word on the right that is most opposite to the word on the left.**

With this question type, you need to match the words given against the word on the left to see if they are opposite. Here is the working out for the example above:

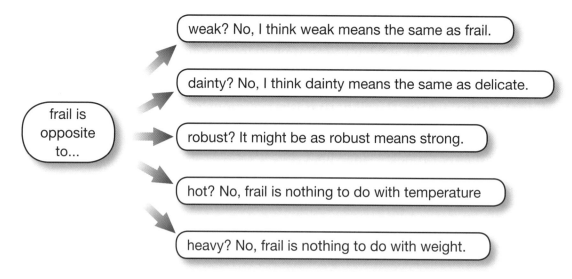

Now I have considered each option, I am confident that the word most opposite to 'frail' is 'robust'.

Q. Underline the one word on the right that is most similar to the word on the left.

With this question type, you need to match the words given against the word on the left to see whether they are similar using the same matching process. Here is the working out for the example above:

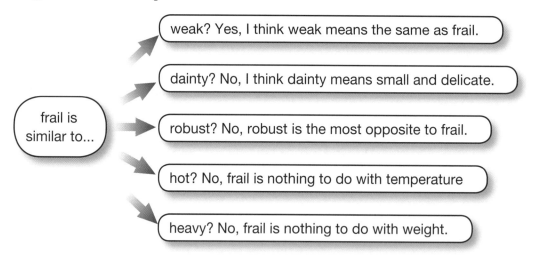

Now that I have considered each option, I can feel confident that the word most similar to 'frail' is 'weak'.

REMEMBER!

Systematic working through of each word allows you to find the most suitable word, but it is also useful if you need to make an educated guess. You may be able to reject some words, leaving you with fewer options to take into account. In any exam, this type of question could take a range of formats so remember that this sorting and matching technique can help whatever the question asks for.

> Q. Add the missing letters to the word on the right to make a word that is opposite/similar in meaning to the word on the left.

Now, this question type can be harder as there appear to be limitless options to choose from, but there are some clever questions that you can use to make the answer less open:

Do you know the word on the left? If so, it can be much easier to work out a word that is most similar or opposite to it.

Can you find a word that fits with the letters that you have been given?

Can we find our word?

Can you use your knowledge of spelling strings to fill in some of the missing letters?

Can you use your knowledge of vowels and consonants to fill in some of the missing letters?

Spelling string technique

Here are some common spelling strings and some words with missing letters. The answers are listed at the bottom of this page, so cover them up and see how many you can get right. Not all of the spelling strings will be used.

er	kn	wh	sh	ch	
str	ough	and	igh	ous	ing
eau	edg	idg	str	est	ful

1 _ _ o w l _ _ _ e   4 s l e _ _ _   7 b r _ _ _ _ t

2 s _ _ _ w i _ _   5 b r _ _ _ e   8 f a m _ _ _

3 b _ _ _ t i _ _ _   6 _ _ a r _ _ _   9 _ _ a t e v _ _

Did you manage to find all the answers?

1 *knowledge*	4 *sleigh*	7 *brought*
2 *sandwich*	5 *bridge*	8 *famous*
3 *beautiful*	6 *sharing*	9 *whatever*

Vowels and consonants

In addition to spelling strings, you can use your knowledge of vowels and consonants to help find an answer. Here are some points to help you:

Checklist

✓ The most common vowel to end words is an 'e'.

✓ The most common consonant to end words is an 's'.

✓ Other common consonant endings include: 'd', 'r', 'ng', 'nd', 'ght', 'l' and 'n'.

✓ Some consonants that begin a word are nearly always followed by a vowel, such as 'q', 'z', 'j', 'h', 'l', 'm', 'n', 'r', 'v', 'x' and 'y'.

✓ The most common vowel pairs are: 'ai', 'au', 'ea', 'ee', 'ei', 'ia', 'ie', 'io', 'oa', 'oe', 'oi', 'oo', 'ou', 'ua', 'ue', 'ui'.

Here are some typical 'words most opposite' and 'words most similar' questions for you to try:

Now it's your turn!

9 Underline the one word on the right that is most opposite to the word on the left. (1)

portable   convenient / moveable / fixed / fluid / spacious

10 Underline the one word on the right that is most similar to the word on the left. (1)

organised   waiter / ordered / system / untidy / chaotic

11 Add the missing letters to the word on the right to make a word that is opposite in meaning to the word on the left. (1)

whisper   b ___ ___ l ___ w

12 Add the missing letters to the word on the right to make a word that is similar in meaning to the word on the left. (1)

placid   p e ___ c ___ f ___ ___

13 Underline the one word on the right that is most opposite to the word on the left. (1)

stylish   chic / fashionable / dirty / old / dowdy

14 Underline the one word on the right that is most similar to the word on the left. (1)

insufficient   lacking / liking / plenty / profuse / average

15 Add the missing letters to the word on the right to make a word that is opposite to the word on the left. (1)

frivolous   e a r ___ ___ ___ ___

16 Add the missing letters to the word on the right to make a word that is similar in meaning to the word on the left. (1)

foe   e ___ e ___ ___

17 Underline the one word on the right that is most similar to the word on the left. (1)

dizzy   fizzy / furious / faint / fresh / ferocious

18 Underline the one word on the right that is most similar to the word on the left. (1)

blighted   wrecked / friendly / attached / grateful / graceful

19 Add the missing letters to the word on the right to make a word that is similar in meaning to the word on the left. (1)

solid   c o ___ p ___ c ___ e ___

20 Add the missing letters to the word on the right to make a word that is similar in meaning to the word on the left. (1)

safer   h ___ ___ m ___ ___ s s

21 Underline the one word on the right that is most similar to the word on the left. (1)

check   change / verify / argue / organise / encircle

22 Underline the one word on the right that is most similar to the word on the left. (1)

transport   remain / return / forge / convey / bicycle

REMEMBER!

If you are still struggling with one of these questions, see whether you can make an educated guess at the word. You might not know the word, but using spelling strings and vowel/consonant knowledge can help you to guess. You might find the correct answer without realising it and any guess is better than leaving a blank.

You might get a word with missing letters, a missing prefix, a missing suffix or you may have a choice of words. Even if you have to just name an opposite or most similar word, these techniques can help you.

E *Words matching pairs of words*

Here is a typical words matching pairs question type:

> **Q. Which word on the right fits equally well with both pairs of words on the left?**
>
> screw, bolt   claw, talon   (spanner, tool, <u>nail</u>, hook, scratch)

In this example, a nail is a type of fixing, so it will fit with screw and bolt. A nail is also a body part like a claw and a talon. Here is a useful technique for this question type:

1 Look at the first pair of words and match each against the words on the right. Any words that fit with this pair, leave in place, any words that definitely do not fit with this pair, cross out.
2 Match the second pair of words with the words on the right that remain.

3 If you cannot find a suitable word, check whether the words have more than one meaning and try the technique again.

4 If you still cannot find the word, then at least you may be able to take an educated guess if there are some words that you have been able to eliminate.

Here is this technique used in the question example above:

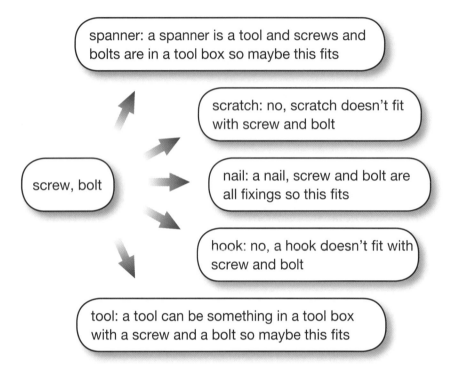

Now we've sorted the first stage so we can reject some of these and match those left over like this:

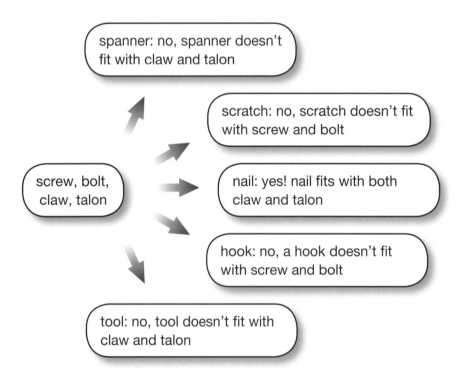

Here are some matching pair questions for you to try:

F   Odd words out

Finding two odd words out is a common question type. Let's have a look at a typical question:

Q. Underline the two odd words out.

    pail   <u>water</u>   bucket   <u>flowers</u>   basket

Q. Underline the two odd words out.

    goose   <u>kitten</u>   duckling   <u>puppy</u>   cygnet

With this type of question, you have to look at how three of the words fit together in order to find the two words that do not fit. Here is a technique that can help you with this question:

1 Find any two words that have something in common and look at the connection between these two words.

2 Can you now find another word that will fit with these two?

3 Once you have three words, the two words that are left will be the odd ones out.

If you struggle to find a connection, see whether you can find another two words that have something in common and try the process again.

Here is the technique worked through with the questions above:

Pail and bucket are both used to hold things in.

Water: No – water is what you put into a pail or bucket.

Flowers: No – flowers are what you might put into a pail or bucket.

Basket: Yes! A basket is something we can put things into.

> **Conclusion: We now know that our odd words are water and flowers.**

Goose and kitten are both baby animals.

Duckling: Yes, a duckling is also a baby animal.

Puppy: Yes, a puppy is also a baby animal.

Cygnet: Yes, a cygnet is also a baby animal.

> **Conclusion 1: We have the wrong connection, as all of these words are baby animals.**

Goose and duckling are both baby birds.

Kitten: No, a kitten is not a baby bird.

Puppy: No, a puppy is not a baby bird.

Cygnet: Yes, a cygnet is a baby bird.

> **Conclusion 2: Now we do have the correct connection, so we know that our odd words are kitten and puppy.**

REMEMBER!

Remember that you are looking for a strong connection for the three words, so if you are unsure of the connection or if the connection is a weak one, try again and see whether you can spot a better connection.

Here are some questions for you to try:

Now it's your turn!

Underline the two odd words out. (11)

28	battle	soldier	fight	captain	conflict
29	jump	canter	trot	gallop	fly
30	solidify	liquidise	set	melt	soften
31	audience	shoppers	boss	secretary	congregation
32	confuse	clarify	explain	perplex	bewilder
33	cultivated	savage	trimmed	wild	natural
34	fan	breeze	buff	wind	supporter
35	cheese	yoghurt	dairy	cow	cream
36	fragrant	perfumed	odious	scented	unkind
37	hexagon	square	rectangle	trapezium	triangle
38	urban	gradient	slope	incline	rural

✓ PARENT TIP

Try the 'Odd word out' game to help your child with these question types. Ask your child, 'What is the odd one out and why?' Then find three words, two of them connected, and encourage your child to find the right answer. Begin with easy ones such cat, dog, monkey (pets versus wild or zoo animal) and work up to harder ones such as almond, hazel, pear (nuts versus fruit). You can make them as difficult as your child can handle and although there are only three words in this game, it is building skills in recognising why one word is different to another and what connections there are between words. Getting your child to make some up for you is equally useful, as they are using the same skills to find connections.

(G) *Logical reasoning*

With these questions, you have to take as much information as possible from a short extract in order to find the solution. Here are some examples of these question types:

Q. Read the following information and then answer the question.

There are five house rabbits: Alice, George, Rose, Sybil and Lucky. Sybil has a nice blue collar. George has a blue collar but he also has a silver bell. Alice has a silver bell and she is a black rabbit. Lucky is also black, but her collar is blue. Rose has a gold bell and she is a white rabbit, but all of the other rabbits are black. Sybil has a gold bell. Three rabbits have silver bells. Two rabbits have red collars.

Who has a red collar and a gold bell? _Rose_

Q. Read the following information and then underline the correct answer.

There are two items on each shelf. The pasta is one shelf lower than the sugar, which is three shelves above the coconut. The pineapple is one shelf above the biscuits and one shelf below the rice, which is one shelf lower than the jam. The flour is on a lower shelf than the biscuits. The tomatoes are the same distance away from the sugar as they are from the beans and the beans are lower than the pasta and the coconut.

Fill in the correct items on each shelf:

sugar	jam
pasta	rice
tomatoes	pineapple
biscuits	coconut
flour	beans

To solve these question types, you need to work step by step through the information in order to gain as much information as you can. You can work through both of these logic questions by using this technique:

For the first question, you need to set out a grid like this:

	blue collar	silver bell	black rabbit	white rabbit	gold bell	red collar
Alice						
George						
Rose						
Sybil						
Lucky						

Then you can work through each piece of information and place a tick in the right place.

	blue collar	silver bell	black rabbit	white rabbit	gold bell	red collar
Alice		✓	✓			✓
George	✓	✓	✓			
Rose				✓	✓	✓
Sybil	✓		✓		✓	
Lucky	✓	✓	✓			

Now that you have everything added in, it is easy to find the answer.

For the second question, you need to create a grid that represents the shelves, and place all of the items on it based on the information that then have. In order to show you the working out in the table, the dark ticks have been reduced to pale when they no longer fit the information, but you can cross them out as you go.

There are two items on each shelf. The pasta is one shelf lower than the sugar, which is three shelves above the coconut.

pasta	flour	beans	sugar	tomato	pineapple	biscuit	coconut	rice	jam
			✓						
✓			✓						
✓			(✓)				✓		
(✓)			(✓)				✓		
(✓)							✓		

The pineapple is one shelf above the biscuits and one shelf below the rice, which is one shelf lower than the jam. The flour is on a lower shelf than the biscuits.

pasta	flour	beans	sugar	tomato	pineapple	biscuit	coconut	rice	jam
			✓		(✓)			(✓)	✓
✓			(✓)		(✓)	✓		✓	✓
(✓)	✓		(✓)		✓	✓	(✓)	✓	
(✓)	✓		(✓)		✓	✓	✓		
(✓)	✓					(✓)	(✓)		

The tomatoes are the same distance away from the sugar as they are from the beans and the beans are lower than the pasta and the coconut.

pasta	flour	beans	sugar	tomato	pineapple	biscuit	coconut	rice	jam
			✓		✓			✓	✓
✓			✓	✓	✓	✓		✓	✓
✓	✓	✓	✓	✓	✓	✓	✓	✓	
✓	✓	✓	✓	✓	✓	✓	✓		
✓	✓	✓				✓	✓		

Now you can start back at the beginning to filter through the information again. There are two items on each shelf. The pasta is one shelf lower than the sugar, which is three shelves above the coconut. The pineapple is one shelf above the biscuits and one shelf below the rice, which is one shelf lower than the jam. The flour is on a lower shelf than the biscuits. The tomatoes are the same distance away from the sugar as they are from the beans and the beans are lower than the pasta and the coconut.

pasta	flour	beans	sugar	tomato	pineapple	biscuit	coconut	rice	jam
			✓		✓			✓	✓
✓			✓	✓	✓	✓		✓	✓
✓	✓	✓	✓	✓	✓	✓		✓	
✓	✓	✓	✓	✓	✓	✓	✓		
✓	✓	✓				✓	✓		

Now you can see which two items are on each shelf to be able to answer the question:

pasta	flour	beans	sugar	tomato	pineapple	biscuit	coconut	rice	jam
			✓						✓
✓								✓	
				✓	✓				
						✓	✓		
	✓	✓							

sugar	jam
pasta	rice
tomato	pineapple
biscuits	coconut
flour	beans

REMEMBER!

Remember to concentrate on every piece of information and work through systematically. If you cannot find the answers, keep reading through the extract, making sure that you make full use of each piece of information.

Here are some logic questions for you to try:

Now it's your turn!

The farmer is sorting out a new layout for her animals. She knows that the cows need a barn close to the field. The pigs eat kitchen waste so it makes sense to put them near the farmhouse. The sheep will follow anyone anywhere so they can be in the middle of the other animals but the goats are often in a bad mood so they have been placed in a higher numbered barn than the cows, and away from the farm house. The donkeys get on well with horses so they are all next to each other. As the horses are often out, they are best near to the farm house and are in the lower numbered barn.

39 Where do all of the animals fit? Place them in each barn. (6)

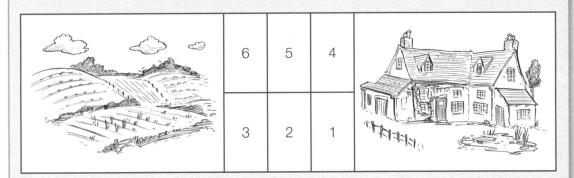

1 _____ **2** _____ **3** _____

4 _____ **5** _____ **6** _____

Jasmine, Kamal, Laila, Meeta and Namar are best school friends. Jasmine sits next to Kamal in French and she sits next to Meeta in science. Namar sits next to Laila in English and next to Meeta in history. Laila sits next to Meeta in maths and in art.

40 Which two girls study science? (1)

_____

41 In how many subjects does Kamal get to sit next to a friend? (1)

_____

42 In how many subjects does Meeta get to sit next to a friend? (1)

_____

43 Which friends does Namar sit next to? (1)

_____

44 Next year Paul will be three times older than Luke, who was twice the age
of Erica last year. Erica will be 7 next year, so how old is Paul now? (1)

_____

Richard, Connor, Dave, John and Pete all like reading. Richard, Connor and Pete like
poetry. Dave, Connor and John like ghost stories and Richard loves drama. Pete,
Connor and Dave like factual books, but Richard and John prefer fiction. Connor likes
books about music and Dave likes books about television programmes.

45 Who likes poetry and drama? (1)

_____

46 Who reads the most types of books? (1)

_____

47 Who likes ghost stories and factual books? (1)

_____

☀ REMEMBER!

Logic questions like these sound so confusing when you first read them, so take a deep breath and
break the question into sections – use brackets if it helps. Now work out each section bit by bit and
you may be surprised at how good you become at these!

How Did You Do?

In this section there were 60 marks available in the 'Now it's your turn' exercises.
Check your answers against the list on page 97. How many did you score?

- 50 or fewer correct? Work through the question types again and make sure that
  you fully understand each section. Once you have done this, try the questions
  again before you move on.

- 51 correct or more. Well done! Do check any questions that were incorrect
  and make sure you understand where you made mistakes and why. Here is a
  vocabulary test with a mixture of question types for you to try:

Practice Test

CEM English and Verbal Reasoning

Read the instructions carefully.

This paper is designed to be completed in **45 minutes**, but the aim is to achieve as many correct answers in the time available. It may not be possible for you to complete every question in the time given, but working through the books that accompany this range will give you the opportunity to work to time and to gain the experience of each question type.

OXFORD
UNIVERSITY PRESS

Great Clarendon Street, Oxford, OX2 6DP, United Kingdom

Oxford University Press is a department of the University of Oxford. It furthers the University's objective of excellence in research, scholarship, and education by publishing worldwide. Oxford is a registered trade mark of Oxford University Press in the UK and in certain other countries

Text © Michellejoy Hughes 2015

Illustrations © Oxford University Press 2015

The moral rights of the author have been asserted

First published in 2015

British Library Cataloguing in Publication Data

Data available

978-0-1927-4288-9

10 9 8 7

Paper used in the production of this book is a natural, recyclable product made from wood grown in sustainable forests. The manufacturing process conforms to the environmental regulations of the country of origin.

Printed in China

Acknowledgements

Page make-up: Oxford Designers & Illustrators
Illustrations: Beehive Illustration

Read the following text and then answer the questions that follow.

Emily's Haven

Life seemed to be a never-ending stream of rushing about; rushing to get dressed in the morning, rushing to eat breakfast, rushing into the car while rushing to school. Lessons seemed to be a never-ending run of the school bell ringing every 40 minutes and moving from the classroom to the sports hall to the canteen to the playground. Emily hated it. She loathed rushing, running, having to be somewhere all of the time. Now it was Friday and Emily wanted to breathe, so here she was plodding along the pavement until she reached the green expanse of grass that ran beside the canal.

Emily slowed down now that nobody was about. She allowed her school bag to drop off her shoulder and it trailed behind her like a forlorn dog. Emily had soon covered the grassland and had a short walk along the canal path until she reached the boat. The narrowboat was painted black with a roof as red as cheery cherries and a smart green hull. It was made of pine and stainless steel with polystyrene insulation making it warm and snug. The traditional boat had three bedrooms inside plus a kitchen, living room with a gorgeous wood-burning stove, a bathroom and separate shower room. To be honest, it looked very much like any other narrowboat that can be found on any canal, but to Emily, it was heavenly and her bedroom was the best place ever.

'Hiya!' she called as she climbed aboard, dumping her school bag in the living room. Emily's grandma held a tray with three mugs of steaming hot chocolate on it. 'How was your day?' she asked. Emily shrugged as she eagerly grabbed her mug. Grandma understood perfectly what Emily's day was like as she had felt exactly the same when she was Emily's age. 'Pop this up to Hannah, will you?' asked Grandma. Emily took the remaining mug and lifted her head out of the cabin. Hannah was on the short back deck sorting through some late blackberries in a silver colander. Although it was mid-autumn, the weather had been beautiful and Emily liked nothing more than blackberry crumble.

Emily sat at the front of the boat sipping her hot chocolate. She gazed out at the hedgerows, wishing that she could live here every day. The usual family of ducks swam up to the boat, hoping for a crust of bread. Emily had watched these ducks grow from ducklings to their present size just as she had watched their parents and their parents before. Emily understood this cycle of nature. Ducks didn't have to dress in uniform or move every time the school bell rang.

'Why should ducks be freer than humans?' Emily thought grumpily.

Grandma was getting supper ready, but there was still time enough for Emily to stretch out on the roof of the boat with her binoculars. She had been tracking a kingfisher that had his nest a little further along the bank. Then a heron family seemed to be watching her, just as much as she was watching them, and Emily could never understand how such a large bird could ever find enough food to eat. The hawthorn hedges on the canal bank produced rich red haws that birds seemed to flock to, along with the purple berries of the elder trees. The holly trees had a mass of bright red berries and there were still blackberries on the bramble bushes, but only in the places that Hannah couldn't reach.

As Emily moved her binoculars around slowly, she could see a quick movement at the base of the hedgerows. Too large for a water vole or shrew, this was more likely a small water rat. Grandma had seen otters many years ago, but Emily had never seen one. It was on her list of things that she would desperately love to see. The sun was now quickly sinking and the air grew chilly. Emily packed up her binoculars and climbed down. Hannah was stoking the stove and the sweet smell of blackberry crumble radiated from the snug little interior. Cheerful lights glowed as Emily settled in front of the stove, pulling an old green and black Welsh blanket around her shoulders, more from habit than feeling cold. Emily would have another two blissful nights before the whole cycle of life began again for yet another long week. The narrowboat stood warm and snug beside the peaceful canal bank, the name of the boat just visible in the failing light: Emily's Haven.

1 What day does this take place on?

_____

2 What was Hannah doing?

_____

_____

_____

3 List four different creatures that Emily sees.

_____

_____

_____

_____

4 Why did Emily wish that she could live on the boat every day? Find five pieces of evidence to support your view.

_____

_____

_____

_____

_____

_____

_____

5   What does Emily mean by the phrase 'cycle of nature'?

_____

_____

_____

6   What do these words mean as used in the text?

    a loathed (paragraph 1)

_____

    b forlorn (paragraph 2)

_____

    c eagerly (paragraph 3)

_____

7   What type of text is this? Find four examples to support your view.

_____

_____

_____

_____

_____

_____

8   The word 'holly' has been written as 'hollies'. What spelling rule is this?

_____

_____

9   Can you find another word in paragraph 5 that has the same spelling rule?

_____

5

2

3

3

1

1

15
TOTAL

10 The word 'stand' has been written as 'stood'. What spelling rule is this?

_____

_____

1

11 Can you find another word in paragraph 6 that has the same spelling rule?

_____

1

12 Why does the author repeat the phrase 'never-ending' in paragraph 1?

_____

_____

1

13 Can you find two similes in the second paragraph?

_____

_____

_____

_____

2

Look at the following words and use them to answer the questions that follow.

alert	bashful	climb	dense	envious
last	gentle	hasty	inside	jealous
kind	last	mercy	nightly	opaque
peaceful	quiet	reply	spite	timid
understanding	vain	watchful	young	zip

14 Find two words that are synonyms for the word 'solid'.

_____

2

15 Find two words that are antonyms for the word 'noisy'.

_____

2

16 Find two words that are synonyms for the word 'shy'.

_____

2

17 Find two words that are synonyms for the word 'aware'.

_____

2

Underline the one word on the right that has the most similar meaning to the word on the left.

Example vision   plotting / smell / <u>sight</u> / style / map

18 crack   egg / cut / shatter / code / delicate

19 sum   maths / add / divide / assume / partial

20 cushion   cover / relax / produce / sheet / protect

Add the missing letters to the word on the right to make a word that is most opposite to the word on the left.

Example ascended   d <u>e</u> s c <u>e</u> n d <u>e d</u>

21 poor   w __ a __ t __ y

22 important   i r __ __ l __ __ a n t

23 smooth   l __ __ p __

Underline the one word on the right that will fit equally well with both pairs of words on the left.

Example smooth, press   brass, aluminium   even / <u>iron</u> / thin / flatten

24 hold, grasp   slide, bobble   clasp / grab / grip / pin

25 file, smooth   train, coach   plane / rub / car / tank

26 heavy, creamy   wealthy, affluent   sweet / weighty / rich / costly

Underline the two odd words out in the following groups of words.

Example purple   lilac   <u>olive</u>   <u>sage</u>   violet

27 coronet   bracelet   tiara   necklace   crown

28 owlet   leveret   leather   hide   fawn

29 pull   push   tug   shove   thrust

30 Read the following information and then answer the questions that follow.

Michael is racing his pet snails Bernard, Brian, Cyril, Harry, Alan and Trevor. He puts them into six starting boxes – A, B, C, D, E and F. Bernard is dozy so he can't be at the two ends or he will wander off. Brian is super-quick so he is in the fast lane at one end. Cyril is between Bernard and Harry. Alan is fast but easily distracted so he is placed at the end of the row next to Harry. Harry is closer to the letter A than Cyril' is.

3

3

3

3

12
TOTAL

Which starting box is each snail in?

A	B	C	D	E	F

Find the three-letter word that can be added to the capital letters to make a new word. The new word will complete the sentence sensibly.

Example We HED the keys to the estate agent. = <u>AND</u> (HANDED)

31 We visited the DETMENT store to buy a school shirt. _____

32 Uncle Paul had a tall tiered cake at his WEDG. _____

33 The theatre had an afternoon PERMANCE of the play. _____

Find the three letters that complete these words. The three letters do not have to make a word.

Example fr<u>esh</u> spl<u>ash</u>

34 peri __ __ __ er   ki __ __ __ etre

35 spa __ __ __ us   me __ __ __ hor

36 c __ __ __ rehend   sc __ __ __ ors

Some of the words in this paragraph have some letters missing. Write out the complete words in the box on the right, so that the spellings are correct and the paragraph makes sense.

In O_ _ _ _er the clocks are put back by one hour whereas in the spring time, the clocks are put f_ _ _ _ _d by one hour. The aim was to save d_y_i_ht and even though there are b_n_f_ts and problems with c_ _ _g_ _g the clocks to British Summer Time, it is a ritual that many people look forward to.	**37**
	38
	39
	40
	41

Underline the correct word in each of these sentences.

Example She (<u>blew</u>, blue) her trumpet solo in the school (<u>band</u>, banned).

42 I know the train (fair, fare) will be more (dear, deer) than using the bus.

43 Our doctors' (practice, practise) looks after many (patience, patients).

44 We crossed a (stile, style) before reaching the middle (of, off) the village.

Complete each sentence by selecting the best word from the options a, b, c, d or e.

Example People travelling to certain countries need ___*d – vaccination*___ .

    a immunity   **b** certainty   **c** vacation   **d** vaccination   **e** respiration

45 I bought some pretty _____ to make some cushion covers.

    a fabrication   **b** immaterial   **c** clothes   **d** material   **e** beauty

46 The _____ of historic battles allows us to see the drama unfold.

    a hobby   **b** creation   **c** presentation   **d** opera   **e** re-enactment

47 Edinburgh is the Scottish capital and is _____ as a World Heritage Site.

    a recognised   **b** reputed   **c** suggested   **d** implied   **e** applying

48–50 The words in the box are missing from the paragraph. Using all of the words, and using them only once, complete the paragraph so that it makes sense.

community	generations	history	nomadic	passed	traditions

5

3

3

11
TOTAL

Within the traveller _____, there are many different cultures from the Circus Travellers, Bargee People and Fairground Show-people to the Roma Travellers, the Irish and Scottish Travellers and Free Festival or New Age Travellers. Much _____ of each group has been _____ down through the _____ by storytelling and song. Country Fairs have been a place where _____ Travellers can come together to meet, to show and sell their crafts and to share their

_____.

3

Read the following sentences and answer the questions.

Example 'The plane's departure time was 13:45.'

What does the word 'departure' mean? Answer: **b**

   a arriving   **b** <u>leaving</u>   **c** resting   **d** mending

51 'The science teacher used a range of lab equipment to perform the experiment.'

What does the word 'range' mean?

   a make   **b** variety   **c** average   **d** example

What does the word 'perform' mean?

   a implement   **b** watch   **c** hear   **d** ruin

52 'Reggae music is a genre that comes from Jamaica and has its roots in Ska music.'

What does the word 'genre' mean?

   a dance   **b** sound   **c** category   **d** song

What does the word 'roots' mean?

   a plant   **b** style   **c** origins   **d** beat

53 'Megan had a summer job of running errands and serving customers in the shop.'

What does the word 'serving' mean?

   a helping   **b** portioning   **c** sharing   **d** selling

54 'The party was very subdued and not at all like the previous occasion.'

What does the word 'subdued' mean?

   a loud   **b** quiet   **c** enjoyable   **d** boring

55 'The house opposite had been vacant for a few months now.'

What does the word 'vacant' mean?

   a dirty   **b** scruffy   **c** empty   **d** rented

5

8
TOTAL

Rearrange these words to make the longest sentence you can. Underline the word that is superfluous.

Example So cream <u>eat</u> the were cakes delicious.

The cream cakes were so delicious.

56 The gently storm child float the little boat watched toy.

_____

57 The film was the about to take the actor in lead the.

_____

58 America is a London city in large Sacramento.

_____

3

Write the plural version of the words in these sentences.

Example Where are the <u>cats</u> (cat)?

59 The chiropodist looked at his _____ (foot) as they were painful.

60 There were three _____ (brush) in the artist's bag.

61 The _____ (reindeer) were ready to pull the sleigh.

62 We like to visit _____ (library) when we go on our holidays.

4

What is the root word in these words?

Example unhappiness   happy

63 deactivated   _____

64 rearranging   _____

65 misinformed   _____

66 impolite   _____

4

Read the following sentence and then find one example of each word class to complete the table below.

Jodie and Kayleigh rode their white ponies at the village gymkhana.

67	proper noun	
68	common noun	
69	adjective	
70	verb	
71	pronoun	

◯ 5

Rewrite these sentences so that they are in the past tense using the fewest number of words.

72 Philip is writing a book.

_____

73 Jon is kicking the football.

_____

74 Louisa is thinking about the party.

_____

75 Janice is standing by the telephone.

_____

◯ 4

◯ 9
TOTAL

END OF TEST

◯ 90
TOTAL

Vocabulary test

Look at the following words and then use them to answer the questions that follow.

crockery	etch	margin	draw	invade
scratch	cookie	scrub	dangerous	mast
suppress	scour	vanity	begin	surgery
post	venomous	commence	dismay	blend
revise	shame	gutter	poisonous	beneficial

1 Find two synonyms for the word 'pillar'.

_____ ◯ 2

2 Find three antonyms for the word 'harmless'.

_____ ◯ 3

3 Underline the one word on the right that is most opposite to the word on the left.

slack   loose / open / tight / melt / solidify   ◯ 1

4 Underline the one word on the right that is most similar to the word on the left.

malicious   delicious / spiteful / precious / wonderful / petty   ◯ 1

5 Add the missing letters to the word on the right to make a word with the most similar meaning to the word on the left.

porous   a b s o ___ b ___ n ___   ◯ 1

6 Add the missing letters to the word on the right to make a word with the most opposite meaning to the word on the left.

mature   c h i ___ d ___ s ___   ◯ 1

7 Which word on the right fits equally well with both pairs of words on the left?

talk, lecture   home, place   (lesson, lessen, part, address, location)   ◯ 1

8 Which word on the right fits equally well with both pairs of words on the left?

adjacent, near   shut, lock   (next, about, zip, close, snap)   ◯ 1

9 Underline the two odd words out.

cardigan   sleeve   cuff   jacket   hem

⟨ 1 ⟩

10 Underline the two odd words out.

float   sink   drop   drift   glide

⟨ 1 ⟩

11 Beth, Brooke, Grace, Lou, Megan and Zara are 5, 6, 7, 7, 8 and 9 but not in that order. Brooke is older than Zara but not as old as Lou. Grace is older than Lou but she is not the oldest girl. Megan is two years older than Beth and Beth is one year older than Brooke. Who are the twins?

_____

⟨ 1 ⟩

Read the following information and then write the correct answers.

At Trinity High School the teachers went to their classrooms for the new academic term. Mr Bell is in the classroom between Mr Whistle and Mr Bat. Mr Bat is not in one of the middle classrooms and neither is his friend Mr Ball. Mr Biter works in a classroom at the end of the row and he is next to Mr Barker, who is next to Mr Whistle. Mr Bat teaches maths.

12–17   Which teacher is in which classroom?

| PE | Maths | English | Science | History | Art |

PE	Maths
English	Science
History	Art

⟨ 6 ⟩

⟨ 20 ⟩
TOTAL

3 Cloze tests

The key areas in cloze tests are:

- find the three letter word
- find the three letters
- complete a word
- contextual words
- selecting words in sentences
- selecting words in paragraphs
- vocabulary understanding
- superfluous words.

Cloze tests are looking for words that fit into a sentence. You may think that sounds easy enough, but of course it is not always that simple! Some of the question types can be tricky to solve as they require not only knowledge of words, but how words change in context. Difficulties can arise in recognising a word when letters are missing and being able to evaluate which words are needed for a sentence to function and to find a superfluous word. Here we will look at the key areas of cloze tests and as each area requires a specific skill, we'll look at how you can develop the skills needed to answer the questions.

(A) Find the three-letter word

In these question types, we have to find a three-letter word that will fit with the given letters to form a proper word that makes sense in the context of the sentence. Here is an example of this question type:

> **Q. Find the three-letter word that can be added to the letters in capitals to make a new word. The new word will complete the sentence sensibly.**
>
> The Black Country Museum is a fascinating glimpse of our TORY.
>
> _____
>
> *HIS – The Black Country Museum is a fascinating glimpse of our HISTORY.*
>
> David ate his supper after he had played with his FRIS. _____
>
> *END – David ate his supper after he had played with his FRIENDS.*
>
> Megan wanted to go to her best friend's PY but she had to go out.
>
> _____
>
> *ART – Megan wanted to go to her best friend's PARTY but she had to go out.*

⚡ REMEMBER!

With this question type, you can place your three-letter word at the beginning, the end or anywhere in the middle of the letters in capitals, but you cannot break the three-letter word up.

Below are a few ideas for finding your three-letter word:

Finding the three-letter word

CONTEXT: Read the sentence and try to work out what the word might be. By finding as many words as possible, it may lead us to the word that we are after.

SPELLING KNOWLEDGE: Look at the group of capital letters to work out what the three-letter word might begin or end with. If your three-letter word is following a 'Q', you know that the three-letter word begins with 'U'. Likewise, if the last letter is 'G', the three-letter word may end 'IN'.

SPELLING LOGIC: Look at the group of capital letters to work out where the three-letter word might fit. If you find a 'Q' next to a 'Z', you can be sure that the three-letter word is in the middle of them.

REMEMBER!

Sometimes the problem with this question type is not finding the correct word; it is knowing how the word is spelled. Try writing the word out and make sure that the three letters do make a real word. Seeing a word in your own handwriting is another way of recognising whether the word 'looks' right or not.

Here are some three-letter word questions for you to try:

Now it's your turn!

Find the three-letter word that can be added to the letters in capitals to make a new word. The new word will complete the sentence sensibly. (8)

1 The mirror on the bedroom wall needed STRAIGHING. _____

2 Our alphabet is divided into vowels and CONANTS. _____

3 REAG books is a great way to improve vocabulary. _____

4 The WHER was not so warm on Thursday. _____

5 We went on HOAY to Turkey this year. _____

6 We love to watch dancing PROGMES on television. _____

7 After digging the GAR my back ached. _____

8 I love VEABLE curry with rice. _____

REMEMBER!

Although there are close to a thousand three-letter words in the English language, it is surprising that the same three-letter words are used frequently in these questions. Here are some of the most popular ones that you will come across, which might help if you are totally stuck. You might like to keep a notebook and add extra words as you come across them.

ADD	AGE	AID	AIL	AIR	ALE	ALL	AND	ANT	ARC	ARE	ARK	ART
ASH	ASK	ASS	ATE	AWE	BAD	BAT	BEE	BET	BID	BIN	BOD	BUD
BUT	CAN	CAT	CON	CRY	DAD	DEN	DID	DIN	EAR	EAT	END	EON
ERE	ERR	EVE	FAN	FAT	FIN	FIT	GAG	GET	GOT	HAD	HEM	HEN
HER	HID	HIS	HUT	ION	IRE	KIT	LAD	LED	LID	LOW	MAD	MAN
MAT	MEN	MUD	NET	NOT	NUT	OAR	OAT	ODD	OLD	ORB	ORE	OUR
OUT	OWE	PAD	PAN	PAR	PAW	PEA	PET	PEW	PIG	PIN	PLY	POT
RAM	RAN	RID	RIG	ROW	SAD	SET	SIN	SKI	SON	SOW	SUN	SUP
TAN	TEA	TEE	TEN	THE	TIN	TIP	TON	TOP	URN	VAN	VAT	WAG
WAN	WAR	WAY	WED	WEE	WET	WHO	WIG	WIN	WON	WOO	ZIP	ZOO

B Find the three letters

This question type is similar to the missing three-letter word, except the three letters don't have to make a word and there is only one word given, so there is no context to help you out.

Here is a typical example of a missing three letters question type:

Q. Find the three letters that complete these words.

s t r o n _ _ _ t   p r e c _ _ _ s

ges (strongest)   *iou (precious)*

With this question type, you have to develop both a wide vocabulary and strong spelling skills. You can use the spelling knowledge and spelling logic techniques that you used in the missing three-letter word question types, to help you with these questions. Here is another technique that can help:

1 Place each letter of the alphabet in the first space and then reject those unlikely to be correct, leaving the most likely letters that fit, like this:

| strona | strond | strone | strong | stroni | stronk |
| stronn | strono | strons | stront | stronu | strony |

2 Now that you have all of the options, try choosing the most likely letter to fit in the last space like this:

| strona _ st | strond _ st | strone_st | strong_st | stroni_st | stronk_st |
| stronn_st | strono_st | strons_st | stront_st | stronu_st | strony_st |

3 Now that you have your most likely options, select those that look like potential words and try fitting the final letter in place like this:

| strondest | stronerst | strongest | stroniest | stronorst | strontest |
| stronutst | stronyest |

4 Now you can see that 'strongest' is the answer.

REMEMBER!

Your aim in any exam is to complete the most correct answers in the time given. This technique can be slow so do try to use your spelling knowledge and spelling logic first. However, if you are stuck, using elements of this technique can help you find the missing letters. For example, if you know that the first space must be a vowel, it cuts down the options to five, which helps enormously.

✔ PARENT TIP

Encouraging your child to work to time is important. Getting one or two wrong answers because they are trying to complete the whole paper to time is far better than gaining one or two extra marks working slowly, but missing out a quarter of the questions because of a lack of time.

Here are some missing-letter questions for you to try:

Now it's your turn!

Find the three letters that complete these words. (8)

9 p u z __ __ __ s   s p e __ __ __ l
10 a q __ __ __ i u m   d o __ __ __ n u t
11 c h __ __ __ c t e r   s a u __ __ __ e
12 p e b __ __ __ s   f r __ __ __ d s
13 f r a __ __ __ o n   m a g __ __ __ n e
14 d i s a p __ __ __ n t e d   u n __ __ __ p y
15 f o r __ __ __ e n e s s   e s p e __ __ __ l l y
16 c r __ __ __ a l s   d i a m __ __ __ s

C Complete a word

This question type is very popular in cloze tests. Here are two examples of complete-a-word questions:

> **Q. Complete each word so that it makes sense in the extract and is spelt correctly.**
>
> 'We have a new n_ _ure rese_ _ _ that has opened up by us. There is a fan_ _ _ _ic lake which at_r_c_s many wild birds and a wide range of h_b_t_ts to su_ _ _ _t a va_i_t_ of wildlife.'
>
> *'We have a new <u>nature</u> <u>reserve</u> that has opened up by us. There is a <u>fantastic</u> lake which <u>attracts</u> many wild birds and a wide range of <u>habitats</u> to <u>support</u> a <u>variety</u> of wildlife.'*
>
> **Q. Some of the words in this paragraph have some letters missing. Write out the complete words in the box on the right, so that the spellings are correct and the paragraph makes sense.**
>
> | It was his first Olympic contest and he was so nervous. Now he stood on the top diving board aware of the whole world w_ _ch_ _g him. He had pra_ _ _ _ed this routine _u_d_e_s of times. He jumped, tucked under neatly and hit the water with pr_c_e_ _i_n. Instinctively he knew it was a gold medal p_ _fo_ _a_ _e. | 1 *watching*
2 *practised*
3 *hundreds*
4 *precision*
5 *performance* |
> | --- | --- |

To solve this question type, you require strong spelling skills and a wide range of vocabulary to recognise words in their context. You can use a mixture of techniques that are also used for finding the missing three letters, such as spelling knowledge, spelling logic and understanding context.

Here are some techniques that might help:

1 Read through the whole extract to see whether the missing letters are obvious. If they are, you have found your answers and can then try and spell the word by adding in the missing letters.

2 Ask yourself what the text is about and whether there are words you know that are connected to it. A few seconds of thinking through words might be enough to generate a list of possible options.

3 Try using your spelling logic and spelling knowledge to solve the words.

4 Sometimes looking at combinations of letters is the only way to solve this question type, especially if there are words that are unknown to you. As always, a guess is better than nothing.

To give you some confidence in working this technique, here is a working out of the extract above to show these techniques in action:

'We have a new nature rese_ _ _ that has opened up.' What fits with 'nature'? Nature park, nature trail, nature walk, nature reserve. This would fit, so **'reserve'** is the second word.

'There is a fantastic lake which at_r_c_s many wild birds.' What is the relationship between a lake and wild birds?

It provides a home for birds because it is attractive. This leads to the word **'attracts'**, which is the fourth word.

'Lake', 'wild birds' and 'wildlife' are all to do with nature and the natural word. **'Nature'** would fit with the first word.

'We have a new n_ _ure rese_ _ _ that has opened up by us. There is a fan_ _ _ _ic lake which at_r_c_s many wild birds and a wide range of h_b_t_ts to su_ _ _ _t a va_i_t_ of wildlife.'

'There is a fan_ _ _ _ic lake.' What begins with 'fan'? What describes a lake? Wet, watery, large, huge, humungous, marvellous, fabulous, fantastic? **'Fantastic'** fits so this is your third word.

'There is a fantastic lake which attracts many wild birds and a wide range of habitats to support a va_i_t_ of wildlife.' Between 'va' and 'i' there must be a consonant: vabi, vaci, vadi, vafi, vagi, vahi, vaji, vaki, vali, vami, vani, vapi, vari

This may now remind you of variety and this would fit. To support a **'variety'** of wildlife.

The word h_b_t_ts shows all consonants, so the spaces are likely to be vowels. If we place vowels between the consonants we have:

Habatats Hebetets Hibitits Hobotots Hubututs

The first 'habatats' may lead you to the word **'habitats'** and this would fit in with the extract, so you have your fifth word.

'There is a fantastic lake which attracts many wild birds and a wide range of habitats to su_ _ _ _t a va_i_t_ of wildlife.' What does a wide range of habitats do? Have lots of wildlife? Keep lots of wild life? Support a wide range of wild life? The word **'support'** fits so you have your sixth word.

REMEMBER!

This question type requires a range of techniques to find the missing letters. Getting used to all of the techniques can help you decide which works best for you and which combination will get you the best results as quickly as possible. The way to really build up key skills is to gain as wide a range of vocabulary as possible through reading, extending your knowledge of spellings and word definitions.

Here are some complete-a-word questions for you to try:

Now it's your turn!

17 Complete each word so that it makes sense in the extract and is spelt correctly. (7)

'During the s___m___e___ holidays we spent a day at the ___e___c___.

We built s___ ___d___ ___st___ ___s and de___ ___ ___ ___ted them

with sea___ ___ ___ ___ls.

We pad___ ___ ___ d in the sea and ate f___ ___h and chips.'

Some of the words in this paragraph have some letters missing. Write out the
complete words in the box on the right, so that the spellings are correct and the
paragraph makes sense. (5)

Traditionally colour is blended by an a_t_st and then applied to the canvas. Pointillism is the technique of p_ _ n_ _ ng tiny dots of paint in pure colour all over the canvas and these dots of colour are 'blended' by the viewer's eye to create shade, s_ _ d_ w, highlight and depth. It is a technique that t_ _ ev_ _ io_ s and computer s_ _ e_ _ s use.	**18** **19** **20** **21** **22**

23 Complete each word so that it makes sense in the extract and is spelt correctly. (6)

The whole park had been turned over to a fe ___ t ___ v ___

wonderland. There were ice-skaters on the fr ___ ___ ___ n ice rink

and little wooden huts sur ___ ___ u ___ ___ ed the skaters selling

ste ___ ___ ___ ng cups of hot c ___ o ___ o ___ a ___ e, roasted

chestnuts and sweet gi ___ ___ erbr ___ ___ d.

Some of the words in this paragraph have some letters missing. Write out the
complete words in the box on the right so that the spellings are correct and
the paragraph makes sense. (7)

In 1990 the Hubble Space T_ l _ s _ o _ e was launched to help sc _ _ nt _ _ ts research the universe. Many di _ c _ v _ r _ es have been made as Hubble helps solve the m _ st _ r _ es of astronomy. Hubble orbits Earth, giving a view of the universe that had previously been imp _ _ s _ _ le. Before Hubble, it was thought that the universe was 10 to 20 billion years old. Now we know that it is between 13 to 14 billion years old. Hubble has also ena _ l _ d astronomers to view baby gal _ _ _ es.	**24** **25** **26** **27** **28** **29** **30**

D Contextual words

These questions require knowledge of words as used in a sentence. Some of the words might not be difficult or unusual words, but they are often homophones, which means that they sound the same as another word but the spelling is different. Here is an example of this question type:

> **Q. Underline the correct word in each of these sentences:**
>
> I don't know (witch/which) parcel to (chews/choose).
>
> *I don't know (witch/which) parcel to (chews/choose).*

You may find homophones tricky because you have to remember which word to use and which spelling is correct. Here are my 'top ten' of the most common homophones that you might come across:

1 Will you <u>two</u> go <u>to</u> the party <u>too</u>?
2 It's a fancy dress party so <u>which</u> of you will dress up as a <u>witch</u>?
3 I don't know what the <u>weather</u> will be like and <u>whether</u> it will stop guests arriving.
4 I should have <u>guessed</u> that another <u>guest</u> would be dressed like me.
5 If we all <u>ate</u> at <u>eight</u> o'clock it would still give us plenty of time.
6 If <u>they're</u> arriving early they could put <u>their</u> coats over <u>there</u>.
7 I should <u>hear</u> you but if you get <u>here</u> and I don't, just come straight in.
8 I've <u>read</u> that <u>red</u> book on 'How to Run a Great Fancy Dress Party'.
9 I can <u>see</u> that you are dressed as a <u>sea</u> creature.
10 I <u>knew</u> that you would wear a <u>new</u> pair of party shoes.

> ☀ **REMEMBER!**
>
> There are hundreds of homophones, so making a list of them as you find new ones will help you to extend your vocabulary. Always try to put them into a sentence so that you know not only the word, but how and where to use the word.

> **Q. She is being so (quiet/quite) that I am (insure/unsure) if she is feeling well.**
>
> *She is being so (quiet/quite) that I am (insure/unsure) if she is feeling well.*

Sometimes it may not be homophones but tricky words or words used in certain tenses that trip us up. Here are some examples of tricky words as used in context:

1 We use 'this' and 'these' or we use 'that' and 'those'.

   This biscuit is good so these are fine, but that biscuit is soft so those are not good.

2 Try putting 'me' into the sentence to work out whether it should be 'I' or 'me', for example, you would say 'I went out' not 'me went out' but you would say 'Can you drive me into town?' not 'Can you drive I into town?'

   Dad followed me into the kitchen, then mum and I baked a cake.

3 We always use 'could have' never 'could of'.

   I could have gone on holiday to the islands of Scotland.

4 'It's' is a shortened form of 'it is' but 'its' means 'belonging to it'.

   It's so funny how that dog hides its bone behind the tree.

5 'Fewer' is used when we are looking at a plural number (fewer bottles, fewer people, fewer sheep, fewer flowers) whereas 'less' is used for something that doesn't have an amount (less time, less food, less than, less money)

   There are fewer cars on the road so people spend less time stuck in traffic jams.

Here are some contextual word questions, using homophones and tricky words, for you to try.

Now it's your turn!
Underline the correct word in brackets so that the sentences make sense.   (8)

31 I (knead/need) to get to the building (sight/site) to meet the bricklayer.

32 Kate, Grace and (I/me) thought that we (had/have) done well with our homework.

33 (Wear/Where) did you say we were (allowed/aloud) to play football?

34 (Shall/Will) we go to the park as (its/it's) not far?

35 Do study in (peace/piece) otherwise you won't (know/no) what to do in your exam.

36 This paint is great, so how do I get that (affect/effect) using (these/those).

37 The car is (stationary/stationery) if the hand (brake/break) is on.

38 They should (have/of) got some (advice/advise) before buying the car.

(E) Selecting words in sentences

These question types require you to select one word from a choice of words that will best fit in a sentence. Here is an example of this question type:

Q. **Complete each sentence by selecting the best word from the options a, b, c, d or e.**

In the summer months we get an _____ of seven hours of sun per day.

a individual   **b** utilised   **c** amazing

d balance   **e** average

e – average

Q. **Complete each sentence by selecting the best word from the options a, b, c, d or e.**

The autumn trees were _____ coloured and vibrant.

a sparkling   **b** many   **c** planted

d richly   **e** dull

d – richly

The technique for solving this question type is to read the given sentence, trying each of the possible words in the sentence and rejecting those that do not fit.

Here is an example of this technique using the question above:

The autumn trees were **sparkling** coloured and vibrant.

This verb doesn't read properly, unless there is a comma to make the word part of a list.

The autumn trees were **many** coloured and vibrant.

This word doesn't read properly here.

The autumn trees were **planted** coloured and vibrant.

This verb doesn't make sense here.

The autumn trees were **richly** coloured and vibrant.

Yes, this adjective works well here and makes sense.

The autumn trees were **dull** coloured and vibrant.

This is an adjective but doesn't work with the word vibrant.

So '**richly**' is the answer: The autumn trees were *richly* coloured and vibrant.

For this question type, the best preparation is to read a wide range of material and to build vocabulary, but there are some hints that can help:

Here are some selecting words in sentences questions to try:

Now it's your turn!

Complete each sentence by selecting the best word from the options a, b, c, d or e. (5)

39 The peacock had such an _____ coloured tail.

    a impressively   **b** impoverished   **c** vitally

    d inappropriate   **e** brightly

40 Rome is the _____ city of Italy.

    a country   **b** county   **c** capital

    d casting   **e** cornerstone

41 My baby brother is very _____, so he is always getting into trouble.

    a boring   **b** quiet   **c** good

    d mischievous   **e** average

42 Our school has a fairly good _____ of books.

    a canteen   **b** class   **c** library

    d teacher   **e** shelf

43 Solar lights work by _____ energy from the sun to power the light in the dark.

    a storing   **b** keeping   **c** protecting

    d preventing   **e** cushioning

F Selecting words in paragraphs

This question type is a case of selecting a word from a choice of those given, to place in a sentence so that the extract makes sense. Here is a typical contextual word question:

> **Q. The words in the box are missing from the paragraph. Using all of the words, and using them only once, complete the paragraph so that it makes sense.**
>
> | aware | fluttering | gardens | lifeline |
> |-------|-----------|---------|----------|
> | native | pollinating | successful | tiniest |
>
> There are many butterflies and moths that are _____ to the UK. Although we see these pretty creatures _____ between flowers, we may not be _____ of just how important they are in both the food chain and in _____ plants. Making sure that our _____ are butterfly friendly is actually one of the most _____ ways in which we can all help nature. Even the _____butterfly friendly plant in a pot could be a _____ for them.
>
> *There are many butterflies and moths that are <u>native</u> to the UK. Although we see these pretty creatures <u>fluttering</u> between flowers, we may not be <u>aware</u> of just how important they are in both the food chain and in <u>pollinating</u> plants. Making sure that our <u>gardens</u> are butterfly friendly is actually one of the most <u>successful</u> ways in which we can all help nature. Even the <u>tiniest</u> butterfly friendly plant in a pot could be a <u>lifeline</u> for them.*

Here is a technique that can help to solve this question type:

1 Read the words that you need to place in the text.

2 Now read the text, ignoring the spaces, so that you know what the text is about.

3 Now reread the text, looking through the list of words as you reach each space until you find one that fits.

4 Once you have finished, reread the extract to make sure that the words you have chosen fit.

Here are some contextual questions for you to try:

Now it's your turn!

44 The words in the box are missing from the paragraph. Using all of the words, and using them only once, complete the paragraph so that it makes sense. (8)

awareness	campaign	dedicated	dignity
illegal	injustice	leading	social

William Wilberforce was a man who _____ his life to

_____ reform, from education and prison reform to public health and

missionary work, but he is best known as a _____ figure in the anti-

slavery _____. It was a difficult task to raise _____

and then support for human _____ for all people and to make people

understand the _____ of slavery. Eventually the Slavery Abolition Act

in 1833 came into place, which would make slavery _____ throughout

the British Empire.

45 The words in the box are missing from the paragraph. Using all of the words, and using them only once, complete the paragraph so that it makes sense. (6)

creatures	developed	playful	sensitive	survive	whiskers

A weather loach is the most gentle of _____. Originating from Asia, they are long, eel-like fish that can _____ for many hours out of water when necessary. They have _____ this amazing ability to cope with swamps, rice fields and muddy ponds that are often stagnant or dried up. Weather loaches love to burrow, dig and hide as they are _____.

They use barbels, which look like _____, to 'see' what is around them and to help them hunt for food. They can be the prettiest shades of golden pink, or duller shades of brown and grey. They are called weather loaches as they are _____ to changes in air pressure and weather.

(G) Vocabulary understanding

Another common exam question that tests your vocabulary knowledge includes sentences or short extracts with questions based on word knowledge. The skill required is not only to know what individual words mean, but how the context changes the meaning. Here is an example of this question type:

Read the following sentence and answer the questions that follow.

> 'The little girl charmed the audience with her song and dance routine.'

Q. What does the word 'charmed' mean?

    a _delighted_   **b** bored   **c** scared   **d** enslaved

Q. What does the word 'routine' mean?

    a habit   **b** _performance_   **c** scheme   **d** tradition

With this question type, you need to look at how the word fits into the sentence. One way of doing this is to read the sentence, replacing the chosen word with each of the words offered to at least reject those that do not fit and to hopefully find the one that does. Remember to look for clues in the other words. For example, here is this technique worked through with the question above:

> **'The little girl charmed the audience with her song and dance routine.'**

'The little girl **delighted** the audience with her song and dance routine.'

If a little girl was singing and dancing she is most likely making the audience happy so delighted would fit and would make sense.

'The little girl **bored** the audience with her song and dance routine.'

It would be possible for the girl to bore the audience, but the word 'charmed' doesn't fit with 'bore'. A charm is lucky, to charm is to enchant, to cast a spell and none of these work with 'bore' so we can reject this option.

'The little girl **scared** the audience with her song and dance routine.'

It is unlikely that a little girl is going to scare the audience with singing and dancing and the word 'charmed' doesn't sound like 'scared' so we can reject this option.

'The little girl **enslaved** the audience with her song and dance routine.'

A snake charmer could enslave the snake but in this context, to enchant or charm doesn't have the same negative effect of the word 'enslave' so this doesn't work here.

Now we can be confident that the word **'delighted'** is the best fit.

> **'The little girl charmed the audience with her song and dance routine.'**

'The little girl charmed the audience with her song and dance **habit**.'

A routine is a habit, but in this context it doesn't work so we can reject this.

'The little girl charmed the audience with her song and dance **performance**.'

Performance fits here – singing and dancing is a performance so this works.

'The little girl charmed the audience with her song and dance **scheme**.'

Scheme doesn't work here. A scheme is a plan and this doesn't work with singing and dancing so we can reject this.

'The little girl charmed the audience with her song and dance **tradition**.'

Tradition could work if the little girl always sings and dances in the same way so it is now a case of choosing which word works best.

Between 'performance' and 'tradition', the word **'performance'** makes the most sense.

REMEMBER!

If you are struggling to work out the meaning of a word, don't forget your word knowledge, spelling knowledge and spelling logic. Is there a prefix or suffix you can take away to leave a root word? Does the word look like another that you have seen or heard? A boy worked out the meaning of a word because it was in the lyrics of a song. He sung the verse to himself and worked out what it meant, so use every single resource that you have.

Here are some of these question types for you to try:

Now it's your turn!

Choose the one word that answers the questions: (2)

'The journalist gained his top story by sitting outside the maternity hospital until the celebrated baby was born.'

46 What does the word 'journalist' mean?

   a reader   **b** celebrity   **c** parent

   d reporter   **e** academic

What does the word 'celebrated' mean?

   a unknown   **b** party   **c** new

   d famous   **e** wealthy

47 'Mrs Pardoe huffed and puffed as she heaved herself up the steep hill.' (2)

What does the word 'puffed' mean?

   a inflated   **b** panted   **c** swelled

   d bulged   **e** snorted

What does the word 'heaved' mean?

   a rushed   **b** dragged   **c** lifted

   d elevated   **e** trotted

(H) Superfluous words

These questions ask you to place jumbled words into an ordered sentence so that you can find the word that is superfluous (not needed). Here is an example of this question type:

> **Q. Rearrange these words to make the longest sentence you can. Underline the word that is superfluous.**
>
> Tea of prefer my milk I cup drink in
>
> _drink:_   _I prefer milk in my cup of tea._
>
> Paddock had donkeys in the tigers the horses and farmer
>
> _tigers:_   _The farmer had donkeys and horses in the paddock._

To solve this question type, the following technique can help:

1 Read the sentence through and then look away.

2 Try to put into words what you think the sentence is trying to say.

3 Look back at the words and try to put them into the order that you thought of.

4 It should now be easier to spot the superfluous word.

REMEMBER!

If this is still tricky, try looking for one or two words that would fit sensibly together and try to build the sentence in this way. Sometimes having one or two words in place and then trying the technique can help. Like most things, the more you practise the technique, the easier you'll find it.

Here are some superfluous word questions for you to try:

Now it's your turn!

Rearrange these words to make the longest sentence you can. Underline the
word that is superfluous. (5)

48 Beat the bagpipes and blew the drums the band marching piano.

_____

49 Eating at the table is outdoors always more eating than exciting a picnic drink.

_____

50 Bunk beds sister room sleep over friends my sister her her when for in has.

_____

51 The cinema theatre moved across the actor of old stage the.

_____

52 Grandpa roasts fire it fireworks on the chestnuts when I love.

_____

✔ PARENT TIP

A good way of helping your child with this question type is to copy out the words of four common nursery rhymes on pieces of paper. Try to make them different and of a similar length so for example: 'Twinkle, Twinkle Little Star', 'Humpty Dumpty', 'Hickory Dickory Dock' and 'Baa Baa Black Sheep'. Also include four obvious words that do not fit into any of the nursery rhymes, for example, 'fire', 'factory', 'protest' and 'fence'. Now mix all of the words together and ask your child to sort out all of the words to form the four nursery rhymes and to find the four superfluous words that are left over. If they can do this, try swapping the four superfluous words for words that could fit in with the nursery rhymes, for example, 'star', 'wall', 'clock' and 'sheep'. Again, mix the words up and see how long it takes your child to find the superfluous words. If you want an even harder version, swap the superfluous words for 'a', 'the', 'for' and 'you'.

How Did You Do?

In this section there were 77 marks available in the 'Now it's your turn' exercises. Check your answers against the list on page 96. How many did you score?

- 65 or fewer correct? Work through the question types again and make sure that you fully understand each section. Once you have done this, try the questions again before you move on.

- 66 correct or more. Well done! Do check any questions that were incorrect and make sure you understand where you made mistakes and why. Here is a cloze test with a mixture of question types for you to try:

Cloze test

Find the three-letter word that can be added to the letters in capitals to make a new word. The new word will complete the sentence sensibly.

1 The chef always SEAED his food with careful balance. _____

2 The laboratory bottles were full of CICALS. _____   ◯ 2

Find the missing three letters that complete these words. The three letters do not have to make a proper word.

3 bo ___ ___ ___ wed   list ___ ___ ___ ng

4 an ___ ___ ___ ams   pige ___ ___ ___   ◯ 2

5–10 Complete each word so that it makes sense in the extract and is spelt correctly.

Poppy used to h___ ___e her wheelchair, but since she has been to training

camp she now loves it. She can rev___ ___se, carry things saf___ ___ ___, get up

and down kerbs and can whiz around cor___ ___ ___ ___. She is even playing

wheelchair bas___ ___ ___ball and wheelchair curling, which terri___ ___ ___s

Poppy's mum!   ◯ 6

Some of the words in this paragraph have some letters missing. Write out the complete words in the right-hand box, so that the spellings are correct and the paragraph makes sense.

At the summer carnival we had a huge b_ _ _ _ y castle, a cake stall, face-p_ _ _ _ing, a tombola, book stall, plant stall and a raffle to raise money for the vil_ _ _e hall. There were floats dec_ _ _ _ed wonderfully and lots of people wore fa_ _ _ dress. We always have a bri_ _ _ _nt time.	**11** **12** **13** **14** **15** **16**

Underline the correct word in each of these sentences.

⬭ 6

17 I had some really lovely (presence / presents) for my birthday and everyone came to my party, which was (grate / great).

18 There (were / where) lots of boat trips leaving from the (key / quay).

⬭ 2

Complete each sentence by selecting the best word from the options a, b, c, d or e.

19 The family _____ his good news with a party for family and friends.

  a admired   **b** remembered   **c** celebrated

  d shunned   **e** forgot

20 Zara used her new sewing machine to _____ a cushion cover.

  a tie   **b** build   **c** knit

  d fashion   **e** utilise

⬭ 2

21–28 The words in the box are missing from the paragraph. Using all of the words, and using them only once, complete the paragraph so that it makes sense.

anticipating	desperately	disturbed	navy
snug	regal	settled	snoring

Gabriel closed the door softly leaving his younger brother gently

_____ in bed. Gabriel had _____ wanted to read

his new book without being _____ and he could only do this when

his brother was asleep. He _____ himself on the bottom step of

the stairs where it was _____ and warm. Gabriel opened the hard

back cover, _____ the message that would be written on the

inside. The dust jacket was a sea of silky smooth _____ blue and

the gold lettering looked _____.   ◯ 8

Read the following sentence and answer the questions that follow.

'The car plant will create over 1500 new jobs, securing the economic
future for the area.'

29 What does the word 'securing' mean?

   a closing   **b** tying   **c** protecting   **d** jeopardising

30 What does the word 'economic' mean?

   a tourism   **b** electric   **c** motoring   **d** financial   ◯ 2

Rearrange these words to make the longest sentence you can. Underline the word
that is superfluous.

31 During bad summer weather we can expect the winter months

_____

32 Cold or warm milk can eat cereal breakfast tea we with

_____ ◯ 2

◯ 32
TOTAL

4 Mixed grammar

The key areas in mixed grammar are:

- singular and plural
- root words
- word classes
- tenses.

Mixed grammar covers a wide range of skills that may arise in the exam. It considers the 'nuts and bolts' of grammar and will provide a solid foundation of understanding. Some of the question types can be tricky to solve as it requires a knowledge of tenses, roots and the spelling rules for plural words. It also requires knowledge of the words classes, which is fundamental for any English examination. Here we will look at the key areas of mixed grammar and as each area requires a specific skill, we'll look at each one and how you can develop the skills needed to answer the questions.

(A) Singular and plural

These question types ask you to either convert singular words to plural, or plural words to singular. Here is an example of these question types:

Q. Write the plural version of the words in these sentences.

The teacher praised all of the _____ (child).

How many _____ (box) do you need to post?

The teacher praised all of the <u>children</u>.

How many <u>boxes</u> do you need to post?

To answer these questions you need to understand how words are spelt in the singular and plural and which words change totally. Here are some of the most common examples that you might find:

Add 's'		Add 'es'		Word changes	
singular	plural	singular	plural	singular	plural
monkey	monkeys	box	boxes	mouse	mice
boy	boys	church	churches	ox	oxen
piano	pianos	bush	bushes	tooth	teeth
house	houses	princess	princesses	foot	feet
sweet	sweets	potato	potatoes	child	children
footballer	footballers	match	matches	goose	geese
car	cars	wish	wishes	man	men
pencil	pencils	bus	buses	woman	women

Take off 'y' add 'ies'		Change 'f' to 'v' add 'es'		Stays the same	
singular	plural	singular	plural	singular	plural
fly	flies	scarf	scarves	sheep	sheep
penny	pennies	calf	calves	fish	fish
spy	spies	knife	knives	deer	deer
poppy	poppies	life	lives	reindeer	reindeer
baby	babies	shelf	shelves	salmon	salmon
puppy	puppies	thief	thieves	trout	trout

Here are some singular and plural question types to try:

Now it's your turn!

Write the plural version of the words in these sentences. (5)

1 Where are the _____ (donkey) and the _____ (sheep)?

2 There are so many _____ (bus) and _____ (lorry) on the road.

3 I have new _____ (shoe) as my _____ (foot) have grown.

4 There are _____ (mouse) and _____ (puppy) in the pet shop.

5 How many _____ (half) of the _____ (pizza) are left uneaten?

B Root words

Some questions may ask you to underline the prefix or the suffix, or to find the root word. Remember that the root is the main word and the spelling of the root can be altered when you add a suffix and prefix to it.

Here is an example of this question type:

Q. Name the root of these words.

silliness = _____

undecided = _____

repainting = _____

silliness = silly   *undecided = decide*   *repainting = paint*

Having knowledge of the most common prefixes and suffixes can help with this question type.

Here are some of the most common ones that you might come across, with their meanings:

Prefix:

ad = towards (advent, adjoin)

dis = not (disappear, distaste)

ex = out or outside of (exhale, exit)

im = opposite to (impossible, impatient)

in = in or towards (inhale, input)

mis = wrong (mistrust, mistake)

non = opposite of (non-fiction, nondescript)

pre = before (preview, prefix)

re = to do again (return, reform)

trans = across or through (transport, transplant)

tri = three (triangle, triplicate)

un = not (unhurried, unplanned)

Suffix:

able = capable of (doable, suitable)

ed = past tense verbs (jumped, liked)

er = adjective for more (smaller, taller)

ess = female (lioness, heiress)

est = adjective for most (nearest, fairest)

ful = full of (wonderful, beautiful)

ing = present tense verb (making, doing)

less = without (hopeless, powerless)

ly = how something is (quietly, friendly)

ous = full of (marvellous, poisonous)

s or es = plural (lads, churches)

y = characterised by (scary, funny)

Here are some root word questions for you to try.

Now it's your turn!

Name the root of these words. (8)

6 transforming = _____

7 immature = _____

8 incapable = _____

9 fashionable = _____

10 hurriedly = _____

11 inactive = _____

12 sensibly = _____

13 helpless = _____

C Word classes

These question types require knowledge of the word classes and how a word within a sentence or an extract can be used. Here are some examples of these question types:

> **Q. Read the following sentences, underlining the words asked for on the left.**
>
> Underline the preposition: The parrot sat <u>on</u> his perch.
>
> Underline the conjunction: The sun was warm <u>so</u> we went swimming.
>
> Underline the noun: <u>Brooke</u> was running far too quickly.
>
> Underline the pronoun: I made lemon cake for <u>them</u> on Sunday.
>
> Underline the verb: David <u>collects</u> seashells.

Q. Read the following sentence and then use the words to complete the table.

Marion and Rachel quietly sat around the wooden table, hungrily eating cherry pancakes.

proper noun =		
common noun =		
verb =		
adverb =		
adjective =		

proper noun =	Marion	Rachel
common noun =	table	pancakes
verb =	sat	eating
adverb =	quietly	hungrily
adjective =	wooden	cherry

For these question types, you need to have knowledge of the word classes, so here is a revision guide that will help you solve these questions.

Nouns

Proper nouns – these are the names, places, dates, titles and words requiring a capital letter at the beginning, for example as 'Monday', 'Mary', 'Medway', 'Mrs Minniver', 'March'.

Common nouns – these are the things and places that don't require a capital letter at the beginning, for example 'cat', 'carrot', 'convoy', 'cup', 'chrysanthemums'.

Collective nouns – these are the words we use for groups of nouns, for example 'team', 'bunch', 'choir', 'flock', 'shoal'.

Abstract nouns – these are the places and things that don't have a physical body, for example 'imagination', 'opinion', 'beauty', 'enthusiasm', 'relaxation'.

Adjectives

Adjectives are words that describe a noun, for example 'old', 'green', 'tiny', 'happy'.

Pronouns

These are the words that we can use to replace a noun, for example 'him', 'her', 'them', 'it'.

Verbs

Verbs are action words, for example 'sit', 'singing', 'stood'.

Adverbs

Adverbs are words that describe a verb, for example 'quickly', 'softly', 'angrily', 'firmly'.

Prepositions

These are words that show us where a noun is, for example 'on', 'in', 'over', 'with', 'of', 'through', 'across', 'above', 'under'.

Conjunctions

These are the connective words joining clauses together, for example 'as', 'or', 'and', 'but', 'so', 'because', 'nor'.

Clauses and sentences

Here is a quick reminder of clauses and sentences, in case you need to consolidate your knowledge of connective clauses:

Checklist

✓ A **phrase** is two or more words put together such as 'little dog' or 'fluffy blanket'.

✓ A **clause** is a group of words that include a verb and could stand alone as a simple sentence, for example 'The sun was hot' or 'Did the boy do it?'

✓ A **simple sentence** that is joined to another becomes a **compound sentence**. For example 'The sun was hot and we had waited all week for it to be dry' or 'Did the boy do it or did he take the blame for her mistake?'

✓ A simple sentence that has a **subordinate clause** added becomes a **complex sentence**. For example, 'The sun, which shone like burnished gold, was hot.' Or 'Did the boy, who has already been in trouble several times this term, do it?'

✓ The main part of the sentence is called the **major clause** and the **minor clause** is called the **subordinate clause** as it is 'extra' to the main part.

✓ If we add description to the verb this is called an **adverbial phrase**, and if we add description to the noun this is called an **adjectival phrase**.

Here are some word class questions for you to try:

Now it's your turn!

Read the following sentences, underlining the words asked for on the left.   (4)

14 Underline the verb: Meera was singing in the school choir.

15 Underline the adverb: We carefully iced the cupcakes.

16 Underline the conjunction: The cottage was quaint and the garden was pretty.

17 Underline the pronoun: Mum was annoyed when she saw the mess.

Read the following sentence and then find one example of each word class to complete the table.   (6)

Matthew had a dream of opening a chain of coffee shops in town.

18	preposition	
19	proper noun	
20	common noun	
21	collective noun	
22	abstract noun	
23	adjective	

Take a different conjunction from the box and place it in a space so that each sentence makes sense. Each conjunction can only be used once.   (4)

and	because	but	so

24 I wanted to play out, _____ the weather was too miserable.

25 The mayor spoke out _____ the crowd remained silent.

26 We spent our summer in the garden _____ the weather was hot.

27 The barn dance takes place on Saturday, _____ there will be nobody at home.

D Tenses

Questions that require us to change the tense of a sentence are popular. Here is an example of this question type:

Q. Rewrite these sentences in the past tense.

Rhys is eating his supper.

_____

Morgan is finding her homework.

_____

Jacob is sitting at the table.

_____

Rhys is eating his supper.   *Rhys ate his supper.*

Morgan is finding her homework.   *Morgan found her homework.*

Jacob is sitting at the table.   *Jacob sat at the table.*

Q. Write the correct tense of the word in brackets in each of these sentences.

The car _____ (turn) into the street.

She will be _____ (wash) the dog at the weekend.

Our friend is _____ (read) a book.

The car turned into the street.

She will be washing the dog at the weekend.

Our friend is reading a book.

For this question type, you need to recognise how the spellings of words change in the past and present tense. There are two forms of the present tense here. Remember the following:

1   The present simple is the basic form of the verb:

I stand, he thinks, she makes, they dance, we talk.

2   The present continuous uses am/are/is and the present participle:

I am standing, he is thinking, she is making, they are dancing, we are talking.

Past tense	Present tense
ate	eat / eating
drew	draw / drawing
slept	sleep / sleeping
ran	run / running
swam	swim / swimming
drank	drink / drinking
drove	drive / driving
watched	watch / watching
thought	think / thinking
bought	buy / buying
brought	bring / bringing
taught	teach / teaching

Past tense	Present tense
stuck	stick / sticking
built	build / building
saw	see / seeing
spoke	speak / speaking
dreamt	dream / dreaming
learnt	learn / learning
sang	sing / singing
felt	feel / feeling
baked	bake / baking
wore	wear / wearing
tried	try / trying
jumped	jump / jumping

Here are some tenses question types for you to try:

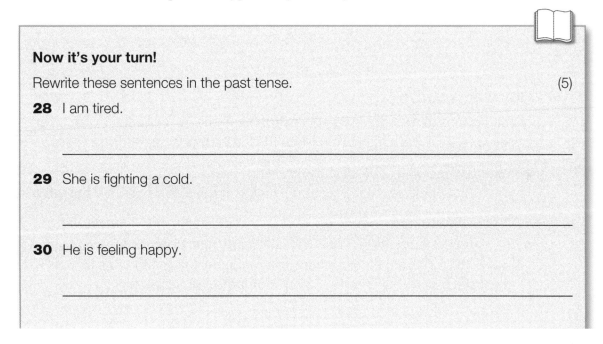

Now it's your turn!

Rewrite these sentences in the past tense.   (5)

28 I am tired.

_____

29 She is fighting a cold.

_____

30 He is feeling happy.

_____

31 They are sailing in a boat.

_____

32 We are peeling oranges.

_____

Write the correct tense of the word in brackets in these sentences. (3)

33 We are _____ (grow) vegetables in the garden.

34 He _____ (tear) the papers into tiny bits.

35 They _____ (speak) to the class of children.

Rewrite these sentences in the present tense. (5)

36 Zara brought some cakes to our house.

_____

37 Dot sold her house.

_____

38 Trevor drove his car to the shops.

_____

39 Chrissy wrote a letter.

_____

40 Dad thought about a book title.

_____

How Did You Do?

In this section there were 40 marks available in the 'Now it's your turn' exercises. Check your answers against the list on page 97. How many did you score?

● 33 or fewer correct? Work through the question types again and make sure that you fully understand each section. Once you have done this, try the questions again before you move on.

● 34 correct or more. Well done! Do check any questions that were incorrect and make sure you understand where you made mistakes and why. Here is a mixed grammar test with a mixture of question types for you to try.

Mixed grammar test

Write the plural version of the words in these sentences.

1 During the winter, _____(snowflake) fall, allowing the
_____ (child) to make snowballs. ◯ 4

2 The row of _____ (snowman) all had stripy
_____ (scarf). ◯ 4

Write the singular version of these words.

3 oxen _____   appendices _____

4 pianos _____   potatoe _____ ◯ 4

Write the root of these words.

5 distasteful _____   counterbalancing _____

6 antifreeze _____   impossibility _____ ◯ 4

Read the following sentences, underlining the words asked for on
the left:

7 adjective   The black cherries tasted sweet.

8 preposition   The submarine sank under the sea.

9 pronoun   Philip loved his sister Chrissy.

10 adverb   The doctor carefully examined her patient. ◯ 4

Read the following sentence and then use the words to complete the table.

'Richard picked the vivid green samphire and cooked it before
nibbling on the salty treat.'

11 Verb			
12 Adjective			
13 Noun			

◯ 3

Take a different conjunction from the box and place it in a space so that each
sentence makes sense. Each conjunction can only be used once.

but	if	because	and

14 You can play on your bike _____ you tidy your bedroom.

15 Beth passed her exams _____ had secured her place at
secondary school.

16 The water was so cold _____ we still paddled in the sea.

17 Egypt in a popular holiday destination _____ the pyramids
attract tourists. ◯ 4

Rewrite these sentences in the past tense.

18 I am trying to write a poem.

_____

19 I am eating some cheese.

_____ ◯ 2

Write the correct tense of the word in brackets so that each sentence makes sense.

20 The girl _____ (play) with her building blocks.

21 Mum _____ (buy) a new blanket for our dog.

22 I will be _____ (grow) potatoes in large buckets this year. ◯ 3

◯ 28
TOTAL

How do you prepare for the exam?

With the CEM exam, there is an emphasis on speed and you may not be able to complete the whole paper. There is often a soundtrack to introduce each section and you will then be talked through the section so that you know what you need to do. It is therefore important not to panic, but to work quickly and efficiently. Here are some tips to help with this:

1 Read the question carefully so that you know what to do.

2 Focus on what the question is asking so that you are precise the first time round.

3 Use a watch or clock when you are practising at home so that you get used to what five minutes feels like or what ten minutes feels like. The *Bond Ten Minute Tests* for English will certainly help with this. The *Bond CEM Assessment Papers* are also broken up into timed sections, which you might find useful.

4 At home, make sure that you know how to perform each technique for each question type, but also make sure that you read the section on 'How to deal with different formats' below for some tips on how to deal with a wide range of question types.

5 Make sure that you read your comprehension text thoroughly the first time round and then scan quickly to find information when you are answering the questions.

6 Never, ever, sit at the end of any section of the exam and wonder what to do. Use every single second to check properly. Redo as many questions as you can to fill in the time. If you are capable of scoring 100 per cent, it would be a shame to miss a mark because you didn't spot the mistake.

> **REMEMBER!**
>
> As with every exam, make sure that you check through your paper and take an educated guess at anything that you don't know. Always use the full amount of time to double check and, if possible, work through some of the questions again to check that your answer is correct.

Effective checking

We always ask you to check carefully but you may not have been shown how to. Here are some tips to help:

- If you have finished the section, check that you have put an answer for every single question. An educated guess is better than a pure luck guess, so try to eliminate any of the options to give yourself the best chance at guessing correctly.

- If all else fails and you cannot eliminate anything at all, then a 'pure luck' guess is better than nothing at all, so try not to leave any blanks at all if you possibly can.

- If you have time and you have already checked that every question has an answer, now work out which of the questions you found trickiest. Go back to them and redo them to see whether you get the same answer. If so, move onto the next trickiest until you either run out of time, or you find a question that gives you a different answer. If you do find a different answer, work out the question again to give you a third possible answer. You hope that the third will match either your first or second attempt. If not, try again until you find a matching answer.

- If you have completed all of your answers and you have managed to work through all of them for a second time, then you have done a thorough check.

- Don't assume that looking at your working out will find the right answer. Always go back to the actual question and begin again from the start as your working out might be problematic.

How to deal with different formats

The types of questions covered here are likely to be similar to those that you'll find in the CEM exam, and many will hopefully be identical but there is always the element of change. This is because the exam board are trying to test how you think, and not whether you can solve a specific type of question. Here is a successful technique to help you with this:

If you place your hand into a 'thumbs up' position we are going to start with the little finger and ask our way up the hand until we reach a 'thumbs up' like this:

4 Can I now go ahead and find the answer?

3 Have I got a technique for solving this?

2 What information have I already got?

1 What is the question asking me to find?

1 **What is the question asking me to find?**

Am I looking for a word, a letter, an anagram, a point of view, a piece of information, some proof?

2 **What information have I already got?**

Do I have an extract to look at, a comprehension text, an anagram, some words to work with, a text type?

3 Have I got a technique for solving this?

Does it remind me of a question type that I have a technique for or is it similar to a technique I have already used? If not can I find a strategy that would work to solve this problem?

4 Can I now go ahead and answer this question?

If so, I have my thumbs up and I can solve the problem. If my answer is 'no', what do I need to go ahead and solve it? Am I looking for clues in the material that I have been given or do I need to think about a strategy for solving this new question type?

GOOD LUCK!

REMEMBER!

You aren't going to be asked to do the impossible so think about the skills, techniques and knowledge that you already have and try problem-solving with these tools. The answer is often far easier that you first thought!

PARENT TIP

The more problem-solving your child does, the easier it is to think in different ways. Board games or computer games of strategy are useful, as are puzzle books that have a range of 'brain training' strategies.

Glossary

abbreviation a word or words that are shortened

abstract noun a word referring to a concept or idea, for example *imagination*

active verb when the main person or thing does the action, for example *she hit it*

adjectival phrase a group of words describing a noun

adjective a word that describes someone or something

adverb a word that describes a verb

alliteration a repetition of the same sound, for example *five funny frogs*

antonym a word with a meaning opposite to another word, for example *wet* and *dry*

clause a sentence with a verb

collective noun a word referring to a group, for example *bunch*

complex sentence a sentence containing a main clause and subordinate clause(s)

compound sentence a sentence containing clauses joined with a conjunction

conjunction a word that links sentences, phrases or words, for example *and, because*

contraction two words shortened into one with the use of an apostrophe, for example *it is = it's*

deduction to look at the evidence and conclude what has happened

definition the meaning of a word

diminutive a word implying smallnes, for example *duckling*

homophone a word that has the same sound as another but with a different meaning or spelling, for example *pain, pane*

inference to look at the evidence and guess what might have happened

main clause a clause in a sentence which makes sense on its own

metaphor an expression in which something is described as being something else, for example *the sun was a gold coin*

noun a word for someone or something

onomatopoeia when a word echoes a sound associated with its meaning, for example *snap*

passive verb when the main person or thing has the action done to them, for example *it was hit by her*

past tense the form of a verb describing something that has already happened

phrase a group of words that act as a unit

plural more than one of something, for example *men*

prefix a group of letters added to the beginning of a word, for example *un, dis, re*

preposition a word that describes where a noun is, for example *on, under, with*

present tense the form of a verb showing something that is happening now

pronoun a word that replaces a noun, for example *him, her, it, they*

proper noun the name of a person, place, date or day, for example *Marion, April, Friday*

reported speech what has been said without quoting the actual words used

root word a word which can have a prefix or suffix added to it, for example *unfriendly*

sentence a group of words that makes sense standing alone

simile an expression that describes something as being like something else, for example *the sun was as round as a golden coin*

singular one of something, for example *man*

spelling rule a rule that we apply to a word when adding a prefix or suffix, for example *reply – take off the 'y' and add 'ies' to make replies*

stanza poems can be divided into blocks of poetry called *stanzas*

subordinate clause a clause that adds additional information to the main clause

suffix a group of letters added to the end of a word, for example *fully, ed, ing*

superfluous an additional word that is not needed in a sentence, as the sentence works perfectly well without it, for example *the handsome man drove the car home*

symbolic something simple that represents something more important, for example the sunny weather could be symbolic for happy times

synonym a word with a meaning similar to another word, for example *smile, grin*

verb an action or doing word

Answers

Comprehension – Now it's your turn!

1 for over thirty years
2 Millie
3 He worked at the zoo.
4 **c** Millie
5 **b** big and fat
6 **c** She owns a hairdressing salon.
7 Mrs Crockett is not a young woman. *Plus any two of:*
   She has 'owned the shop for over thirty years'.
   She has seen 'generations of young children' over the years.
   She has two adult children – Jack works for the zoo and Millie has a hairdressing salon.
   She was 'close to retirement.'
8 Mrs Crockett loves her shop because the text describes her shop as 'beloved'.
9 Yes, toys can influence the career that children have when they grow up because *(plus either of the following)* Jack played with toy animals and he now works in a zoo OR Millie combed her dolls' hair and she is now a hairdresser.
10 No. Plus any one of: The text says that children 'gazed at the fashions of the day'. The text also lists the types of toys that have been popular over the years.
11 Either 'yes' and any one of the following:
   Toy cars are more exciting when they are "racing cars".
   Dolls are more exciting when they are 'talking dolls'.
   OR 'no' and any one of the following:
   Teddy bears, board games and craft kits are always popular.
   Jack had always loved toy animals.
   Millie combed dolls' hair.

12 **a** Gazed means looked/stared/eyed/ marvelled at.
   b Wonder means think/worry about/ consider.
   c Beloved means loved/adored/cherished/ precious.
13 **a** generations OR always
   b fashion
   c close
14 The extract is from a story. *Plus any three of:* the text is written in free-flowing prose, the story is written in the third person, the text has character's names, the extract uses descriptive words, the extract has a plot
15 'talk' has had the 'ing' suffix and needs no change to the spelling.
16 combing
17 'do' has become 'did' as it is a past tense word that has changed its spelling.
18 'has/had' or 'think/thought' or 'will/would' or 'spend/spent' or 'is/was'
19 for (four, fore)
20 **a** generation
   b child
   c doll
21 **a** businesses
   b zoos
   c hairdressers
22 Jack's toy animals show us how much he loved his toy animals and because of this love he has ended up working in a zoo. If Mrs Crockett hadn't owned the toy shop, he might never have had the toy animals and might now be doing another job.
23 The list of toys shows us the huge range of toys that were in the shop

Comprehension test

1 The dispensing optician can offer advice on night driving lenses, sunglasses, safety eyewear, sports glasses and contact lenses.
2 The optometrist can examine eyes, use sight tests, prescribe glasses, prescribe contact lenses, provide advice on various problems, prescribe treatments, refer patients to doctors or medical specialists.
3 An eye-patch over the strong eye forces the weaker eye to become strong.
4 If a baby can crawl, it can turn and move towards the person speaking and this can help a baby to focus.

5 Yes, modelling clay would help because any motor and hand-to-eye co-ordination is recommended.
6 No, I would not agree, because an optometrist can spot eye diseases, disorders and sight issues before they become problematic, they can also prescribe treatment if it is needed and can refer a patient to a doctor or specialist before the problem gets worse.
7 **a** variety = a range of/different types of
   b corrected = put right/cured/solved
   c occasion = special event like a wedding/ party/birthday

8 **a** gallery
    b experience
    c problematic

9 a website *plus any four of the following:* there is a www web address at the top, there are internet buttons to jump to other pages, the writing is in columns and boxes, the writing is informative, the writing is factual, there is a gallery of items to buy, it says 'click here to see our gallery'.

10 **a** 'activity' has been written as 'activities' as it has changed from the singular to the plural so we take off the 'y' and add 'ies'.
    b Another word with the same rule is 'accessories'.

11 **a** The spelling rule is to take off the 'e' before adding the 'ing'.
    b Other words with the same rule are provide/providing, prescribe/prescribing, dispense/dispensing, drive/driving

12 'your eyes are the windows to the soul'

13 'providing proper protective'

Vocabulary – Now it's your turn!

1 dusk and sunset
2 clear and transparent
3 mild and calm
4 messy and disorganised
5 deceive, cheat
6 entrance, entry
7 spin, turn
8 pause, rest
9 fixed
10 ordered
11 bellow
12 peaceful
13 dowdy
14 lacking
15 earnest
16 enemy
17 faint
18 wrecked
19 compacted
20 harmless
21 verify
22 convey
23 space
24 funny
25 slip
26 wave
27 bill
28 soldier and captain
29 jump and fly
30 solidify and set
31 boss and secretary
32 clarify and explain
33 cultivated and trimmed
34 breeze and wind
35 dairy and cow
36 odious and unkind
37 hexagon and triangle
38 rural and urban
39 1 = horses   2 = donkeys   3 = cows
    4 = pigs   5 = sheep   6 = goats
40 Meeta and Jasmine
41 1 (French with Jasmine)
42 4 (Jasmine in science, Namar in history, Laila in maths and in art)
43 Laila (in English) and Meeta (in history)
44 Paul is 35.
45 Richard
46 Connor
47 Connor and Dave

Vocabulary test

1 mast, post
2 venomous, poisonous, dangerous
3 tight
4 spiteful
5 absorbent
6 childish
7 address
8 close
9 cardigan and jacket
10 sink and drop
11 Beth and Lou
12 PE = Mr Ball
13 Maths = Mr Bat
14 English = Mr Bell
15 Science = Mr Whistle
16 History = Mr Barker
17 Art = Mr Biter

Cloze tests – Now it's your turn!

1 TEN (straightening)
2 SON (consonants)
3 DIN (reading)
4 EAT (weather)
5 LID (holiday)
6 RAM (programmes)
7 DEN (garden)
8 GET (vegetable
9 zle (puzzles)   cia (special)
10 uar (aquarium)   ugh (doughnut)
11 ara (character)   sag (sausage)
12 ble (pebbles)   ien (friends)
13 cti (fraction)   azi (magazine)
14 poi (disappointed) hap (unhappy)
15 giv (forgiveness) cia (especially)
16 yst (crystals)   ond (diamonds
17 summer, beach, sandcastles, decorated, seashells, paddled, fish
18 artist
19 painting
20 shadow
21 televisions
22 screens
23 festive, frozen, surrounded, steaming, chocolate, gingerbread
24 telescope
25 scientists
26 discoveries
27 mysteries
28 impossible
29 enabled
30 galaxies
31 need and site
32 I and had
33 where and allowed
34 shall and it's
35 peace and know
36 effect and these
37 stationary and brake
38 have and advice
39 **a** impressively
40 **c** capital
41 **d** mischievous
42 **c** library
43 **a** storing
44 dedicated, social, leading, campaign, awareness, dignity, injustice, illegal
45 creatures, survive, developed, playful, whiskers, sensitive
46 **d** reporter   **d** famous
47 **b** panted   **b** dragged
48 piano – The marching band beat the drums and blew the bagpipes.
49 drink – Eating a picnic outdoors is always more exciting than eating at the table.
50 sister – My sister has bunk beds in her room for when her friends sleep over.
51 cinema – The actor moved across the stage of the old theatre.
52 fireworks – I love it when grandpa roasts chestnuts on the fire.

Cloze test

1 SON (seasoned)
2 HEM (chemicals)
3 rro (borrowed)   eni (listening)
4 agr (anagrams)   ons (pigeons)
5 hate
6 reverse
7 safely
8 corners
9 basketball
10 terrifies
11 bouncy
12 face-painting
13 village
14 decorated
15 fancy
16 brilliant
17 presents, great
18 were, quay
19 **c** celebrated
20 **d** fashion
21 snoring
22 desperately
23 disturbed
24 settled
25 snug
26 anticipating
27 navy
28 regal
29 **c** protecting
30 **d** financial
31 summer – During the winter months we can expect bad weather.
32 tea – We can eat breakfast cereal with warm or cold milk.

Mixed grammar – Now it's your turn!

1 donkeys, sheep
2 buses, lorries
3 shoes, feet
4 mice, puppies
5 halves, pizzas
6 form
7 mature
8 capable or able
9 fashion
10 hurry
11 active or act
12 sense
13 help
14 'singing' is the verb as it is a doing word.
15 'carefully' is the adverb as it describes how we are icing the cakes.
16 'and' is the conjunction to join both clauses.
17 'she' is the pronoun that replaces the word 'mum'.
18 in or of
19 Matthew
20 shops or town
21 chain
22 dream is an abstract noun when used like this (I had a dream)
23 coffee is an adjective here as it describes the shop
24 but
25 and
26 because
27 so
28 I was tired.
29 She fought a cold.
30 He felt happy.
31 They sailed in a boat.
32 We peeled oranges.
33 growing
34 tore
35 spoke
36 Zara is bringing some cakes to our house.
37 Dot is selling her house.
38 Trevor is driving his car to the shops.
39 Chrissy is writing a letter.
40 Dad is thinking about a book title.

Mixed grammar test

1 snowflakes, children
2 snowmen, scarves
3 ox, appendix
4 piano, potato
5 taste, balance
6 freeze, possible
7 black
8 under
9 his
10 carefully
11 picked, cooked, nibbling
12 vivid, green, salty
13 Richard, samphire, treat
14 if
15 and
16 but
17 because
18 I tried to write a poem.
19 I ate some cheese.
20 played
21 bought
22 growing

Standard CEM English and verbal reasoning pull-out test

1 Friday
2 Hannah was sorting through some blackberries.
3 Emily sees ducks, herons, a kingfisher, a water rat.
4 *Any five of:* Emily hated rushing and the boat was calm; Emily hated having to be in certain places at a certain time and she didn't have to on the boat; Emily felt that she could breathe on the boat; Emily loved the peace and quiet of nature; Emily felt free and unrestricted on the boat; Emily enjoyed looking at the creatures from the boat; the boat was a haven for Emily; the boat was a cosy place to escape from her weekly life.
5 Emily has watched baby ducklings grow up and have their own babies. They then grew up and had their own babies, which is a never-ending process.
6 a loathed = hated/detested/abhorred
   b forlorn = sad/neglected/pitiful/lost
   c eagerly = enthusiastically/keenly/excitedly
7 The text is a story. *Plus any four of:* The text is written in flowing prose; the text is divided into paragraphs; the piece is written in the third person; characters' names are used; there is a plot; the writing is descriptive; it is a fictional piece of writing.
8 The word 'holly' is singular and the word 'hollies' is plural.
9 'Blackberry' becomes 'blackberries'.
10 The word 'stand' has become 'stood' because it is written in the past tense and the word changes for the past tense.
11 *Any one of:* can/could, is/was, begin/began.
12 The repetition of the phrase highlights the constant, never-ending nature of Emily's life.
13 Her school bag is 'like a forlorn dog'. The roof of the boat is 'as red as cheery cherries'.
14 dense, opaque
15 quiet, peaceful
16 bashful, timid
17 alert, watchful
18 shatter
19 add
20 protect
21 wealthy
22 irrelevant
23 lumpy
24 grip

25 plane
26 rich
27 bracelet, necklace
28 leather, hide
29 pull, tug
30 A = Alan, B = Harry, C = Cyril, D = Bernard, E = Trevor, F = Brian
31 PAR (department)
32 DIN (wedding)
33 FOR (performance)
34 met (perimeter), lom (kilometre)
35 cio (spacious), tap (metaphor)
36 omp (comprehend), iss (scissors)
37 October
38 forward
39 daylight
40 benefits
41 changing
42 fare, dear
43 practice, patients
44 stile, of
45 d material
46 e re-enactment
47 a recognised
48–50 communities, history, passed, generations, nomadic, traditions
51 b variety   a implement
52 c category   c origins
53 a helping
54 b quiet
55 c empty
56 storm – The little child watched the toy boat gently float.
57 the – The actor was about to take the lead in the film.
58 London – Sacramento is a large city in America.
59 feet
60 brushes
61 reindeer
62 libraries
63 act or active
64 arrange
65 form or inform
66 polite
67 Jodie or Kayleigh
68 ponies or gymkhana
69 white or village
70 rode
71 their
72 Philip wrote a book.
73 Jon kicked the football.
74 Louisa thought about the party.
75 Janice stood by the telephone.

Resources

www.bond11plus.co.uk

The Bond website is a fantastic resource for all things 11⁺.

For the Bond CEM English and Verbal Reasoning the following books are recommended:

CEM English and Verbal Reasoning Assessment Papers 10–11⁺ years

CEM English and Verbal Reasoning Assessment Papers 9–10 years

CEM English and Verbal Reasoning Assessment Papers 8–9 years

CEM Standard Test Papers

CEM Multiple-choice Test Papers

CEM English and Verbal Reasoning 10 Minute Tests 10–11⁺ years

CEM English and Verbal Reasoning 10 Minute Tests 9–10 years

CEM English and Verbal Reasoning 10 Minute Tests 8–9 years

CEM English Word Problems 10 Minute Tests 10–11⁺ years

CEM English Comprehension 10 Minute Tests 10–11⁺ years

CEM English Vocabulary 10 Minute Tests 10–11⁺ years

Bond English Ten Minute Tests 9–10

Bond English Ten Minute Tests 10–11⁺

Focus on Comprehension

Bond Comprehension 9–10

Bond Comprehension 10–11⁺

Bond Comprehension 11⁺–12⁺